WATER RESOURCES MONOGRAPH   **2**

Benefit-Cost Analysis for Water System Planning

CHARLES W. HOWE

AMERICAN GEOPHYSICAL UNION
WASHINGTON, D. C.
1971

Water Resources Monograph Series

B E N E F I T - C O S T   A N A L Y S I S
F O R   W A T E R   S Y S T E M   P L A N N I N G

CHARLES W. HOWE

Copyright © 1971 by the
American Geophysical Union
1707 L Street, N. W.
Washington, D. C. 20036

First Printing December 1971
Second Printing December 1972

Library of Congress Catalog No. 72-182565
Standard Book No. 87590-302-9

List Price, $2.00

Printed by
PUBLICATION PRESS, INC.
Baltimore, Maryland

FOREWORD

As a result of expanding population and economic pressures throughout the world, interest in water resources has increased greatly in the past decade. This interest has stimulated an expansion of investigational facilities and programs by universities and private and government organizations. There have been rapid advances in data collection, modeling of hydrologic processes, and development planning and management of water resource systems.

How to disseminate the results of this research rapidly concerns both the researcher and the user. To some extent, tutorial and 'state-of-the-art' publications may accomplish this goal by offering critical and well-articulated presentations in depth. Such publications need to emphasize the application of the research results rather than the esoteric nature of the research itself.

The American Geophysical Union continues its publication of the Water Resources Monograph Series with the intention of playing that role. Benefit-Cost Analysis for Water System Planning, the second monograph of this series, is also the second of three monographs designated as U.S. contributions to the International Hydrological Decade.

As far as possible, each monograph will be self-contained and will deal with a specific technique of analysis. The monograph series will offer an opportunity for critical review and implementation of recent research results by those engaged in the day-to-day problems of planning and managing water resource systems.

iii

The preparation and publication of this series is supported in part by funds provided by the U.S. Department of the Interior as authorized under the Water Resources Research Act of 1964, as amended, and in part by a grant from Resources for the Future, Inc.

N. C. MATALAS
Chairman, Editorial Board
Water Resources Monograph Series

PREFACE

This is a small book on a very large topic: water resource system planning. The term water resource system as used here means a combination of structural and nonstructural measures, including rules of operation, for transforming stocks or flows of water into more useful outputs of water, water services, or water-related products. Examples of these outputs would include municipal water supply, flood control, waste disposal and water quality management, navigation, irrigation, and hydroelectric power. Both the original water inputs and the outputs are characterized by quantity, quality, time, and place.

Planning refers to a continuing process over time of making decisions regarding (1) what resources to invest (in the form of capital, operating, maintenance, and repair inputs) on which projects and where these projects will be located, and (2) when these projects should be undertaken. The term project here means something considerably more general than a single structure. A project could mean a set of coordinated structures, structures coordinated with nonstructural measures (such as zoning, flood insurance, and the setting of water prices and waterway user charges), or the design of nonstructural measures by themselves.

Naturally, a project must be designed before it can be fitted into a wider plan or even before it can be considered for inclusion in a wider plan. Thus we will speak of the design of a structure in terms of the height and type of a dam, the spillway, the length of penstocks, the intended allocation of storage to power generation, flood storage,

and other engineering characteristics. We will also speak
of the design of nonstructural tools of management, such as
a plan for floodplain zoning or the design of an appropriate
rate structure for water supply.

The objective of the book is to set forth some of the
basic elements of a broad benefit-cost approach to water resources planning. Clearly, the book cannot cover all aspects
of river basin or regional planning, large-scale economic
projections, or the use of highly sophisticated computer optimization and simulation models. What you will in fact find
here is a framework for project design and selection based
on a recognition that water projects have impacts extending
beyond those capable of monetary quantification and that environmental, esthetic, and equity impacts must be forecast
and described if projects are to be designed and ranked in
order of their contribution to human well-being.

The approach used here is that of the economist, and
the reader will find a heavy emphasis on the quantifiable
goods and bads. To claim that economic analysis can fully
take into account all social concerns or that it can, without interacting with the political process, produce socially
optimal decisions would be a disservice to the reader and
to the discipline. Rather, it is contended that the methods
of economic analysis that are feasible today are powerful
tools for illuminating the ranges of alternatives open to
planners and for describing many of the impacts that water
projects can have. The results of applying the methods of
analysis that are described here are important inputs into
the decision process, especially during periods of tight
government budgets and capital markets.

This book should be useful to water planners and managers at all levels of government, local through federal.
Planners and consultants to private water firms too should
find much of use here even though the accounting stances
and viewpoints that they may be called on to use are

narrower than those appropriate for the public sector.
Problems that are unique to particular levels of government
cannot be treated in detail, but the framework presented will
be readily adapted by the reader to his own decision making
situation.

CHARLES W. HOWE
University of Colorado
Boulder, Colorado

ACKNOWLEDGMENTS

The origins of this book can be traced to a manual for a short benefit-cost course that the author prepared for Robert R. Nathan Associates, Inc. The manual presented a potential foundation for a much more thorough consideration of benefit-cost analysis, so the author gladly responded to the invitation of the American Geophysical Union to contribute a volume on economic analysis to the Water Resources Monograph Series.

I am greatly indebted to the reviewers of the original manuscript who committed themselves far beyond the call of duty to detailed critiques that have resulted in a much more consistent and concise presentation: Harvey O. Banks, Consulting Engineer; Blair T. Bower of Resources for the Future, Inc.; Louis Michael Falkson of Cornell University; Robert H. Haveman of the University of Wisconsin; Robert J. Kalter of Cornell University; Allen V. Kneese of Resources for the Future, Inc.; Jack L. Knetsch, senior staff member on the Council on Environmental Quality; and Gilbert F. White of the University of Colorado.

The author would also like to acknowledge discussions held with Jacob van der Wiel, Alan Schultz, and E. W. Shomo, Jr. when all were working together on water development problems for Robert R. Nathan Associates, Inc. These discussions relating to the application of economic analysis to complex actual planning problems have made this book much more relevant than it could have been otherwise. Discussions with my current colleagues Edward Phillips, Nicholas Schrock, and Reuben Zubrow during revisions of the manuscript helped greatly in settling some of the potential conflicts between the niceties of economic theory and the complexities of actual decisions. Having such generous colleagues is indeed a privilege.

Many thanks, too, for the good humor and excellent typing of Frances Macy and Karen Kibben, who typed the various versions of the manuscript.

CONTENTS

xi

6. CRITERIA FOR PROJECT DESIGN AND SELECTION

7. CASE STUDIES

1 INTRODUCTION

Point of View

This book discusses aids to public decision making, i.e., aids to water managers, planners, and decision makers at all levels of government, local through federal. (The term water manager will be used to indicate water system managers, designers, or an appropriate decision-making group. The context will make clear what the appropriate interpretation is.) This does not imply that what follows is of no interest to water managers in the private sector (privately owned municipal water companies, heavy water-using industries, and so on), but the type of profit calculus required in the private sector is much too narrow a base on which to build appropriate decision procedures for the public sector. If a privately owned water company serves a municipality and is regulated as a public utility in such a way that in making its investment decisions it can count benefits and costs of all kinds regardless of the parties to whom these costs accrue, then this privately owned water company certainly should be counted as a part of the public sector for present purposes, and its managers should be interested in this book.

It will not be possible to treat all the significant problems at every level of government. Certainly the revenue problems of a local government are considerably different from those of the U.S. Army Corps of Engineers, and the range of considerations relevant to the Great Lakes River Basin Commission is considerably broader than that relevant to a water conservation district. Yet it is hoped that a general framework for analysis can be presented in these pages that will be useful to all water managers. Many of the differences in decision-making settings faced at different public or governmental levels concern the so-called 'accounting stance' to be assumed by the manager or by the decision makers to whom the manager is responsible;

1

i.e., Whose benefits and costs are to be counted when making water
development decisions? This topic is treated in some detail in chapter 2.

The public water manager at each level faces a certain institutional framework in terms of the legal definitions of his responsibilities, the legally defined or traditionally set scope of actions
open to him, and the system of incentives and rewards that are important determinants of how he is likely to react to a particular
situation. For example, if a law states or has been interpreted to
mean that the department of water supply is to permit no shortage to
occur, then one should not be surprised if the water manager attempts to avoid all shortages, even if it is economic nonsense to do
so. If the U.S. Army Corps of Engineers is charged with reviving
the economy of a depressed region, one should not be surprised if
they attempt to revive it with dams and reservoirs rather than with
education, retraining, or the development of resorts, whatever the
merits of the latter. If the water manager ignores the downstream
effects of the city's water supply or waste disposal procedures because his rewards are related to minimizing the city's water and
waste costs alone, one should not be too surprised.

It will be the viewpoint of this book that the water manager at a
given level of government will have a natural viewpoint or accounting stance, i.e., a geographical preview over which the various impacts of his actions will be measured. Given this natural accounting stance, his actions are shaped by certain legally determined parameters such as those mentioned above: the definition of responsibility, the scope of actions open to him, the reward structure, and
so on. If the water manager is led by these parameters to act in
ways that are socially undesirable, he alone should not be condemned
for narrow-mindedness. The parameters defining his responsibilities
and rewards should be changed. New public water policies should be
evolved at the appropriate levels. It will not be assumed here that
the local water manager can be asked to take a national viewpoint
unless appropriate policies make the local and national viewpoints
coincide, although we would much encourage the broader point of view.

General Economic Problem: Scarcity

The public, however defined, certainly doesn't have all that it wants of water, housing, food, education, or good environment. The problem is scarcity, i.e., scarcity of at least some of the inputs required for the production of products (e.g., industrial capacity, fuel, wood, grains) or required directly for human satisfaction (e.g., clean air, pleasant natural surroundings, absence of excessive noise). The list of items that are generally considered scarce changes with time, usually by adding new items. Land, water, timber, and mineral resources in their natural settings were once considered nonscarce or free because of the vast supplies available relative to the demands.

Scarcity is most generally registered in the marketplace by price. However, the past decade has shown that air, water, and open space are no longer free and that they are scarce commodities of rising value, even if there are no ordinary markets in which this rise in value is reflected. (Further discussion of the difficulties in establishing markets for these 'common property' resources will be forthcoming in chapters 3 and 4.)

The general economic problem is to use available scarce resources to maximize resultant human welfare. This maximization means that alternative configurations of resource use among types of use, over space, and through time must be compared in terms of the net benefits that the resources will generate, the benefits being interpreted in the broadest possible terms. The real costs of any particular configuration of resource use consist of the benefits that would be realized through other patterns of resource use.

Different types of benefits and costs are generated by a given pattern of resource use. Some benefits and costs are correctly registered in markets by prices, some are incorrectly registered by market prices, some are registered in no markets although simulated market values can be computed, and for others it is nearly impossible to think of any kind of adequate market valuation process. Examples of the above possibilities in terms of benefits might be the market

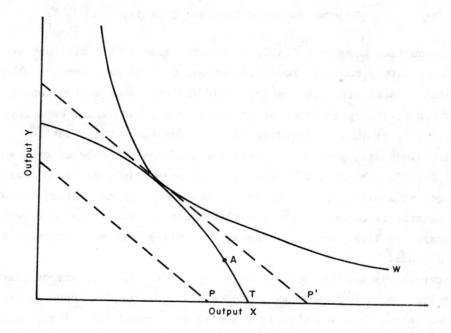

Fig. 1. Social choice of optimum project design.

values of free market-irrigated crops, the price of sugar beets, the
value of recreation on publicly provided reservoirs, and the value
of a beautiful landscape or view.

The economic problem facing any public decision maker can be re-
stated in a simple two-dimensional example. Let X and Y (Figure 1)
represent quantitative measures of two distinct outputs of, let us
say at first, a reservoir: peak electrical power output and reliable
municipal water supply. Let us suppose that a given budget is
available for the construction of the reservoir (although in practice, the budget may not be set until after the design is determined). What can we get with that budget in terms of the outputs?
Generally, there will be a great many different mixes of outputs that
technically can be achieved, each representing a particular trade off
of one output against another. The curve T indicates the different
possible designs.

Who designs the information about the possible alternatives?
Naturally the design engineer must figure out what T looks like.

Designing one particular project such as *A* in Figure 1 is a useful start, but such information alone fails to indicate the range of alternative outputs that could be derived from the given budget. Other output mixes might be more highly desired by society.

Who develops information about the values to be placed on different mixes of outputs? Sometimes the water manager may have to develop his own information. In the case of the two outputs of this example, the valuations might be provided by the existing market prices for power and water if the project provides no further benefits or harm to other parties. The prices can be represented by the price line *P* showing the different combinations of the outputs that could be purchased for a fixed total outlay. The optimum project design could, in this simple case, be determined by finding the point *B* where the highest price line *P'* is just tangent to *T*, because at that point the market value of the project output is highest.

Suppose, however, that the two relevant outputs are hydro-peaking power and environmental-esthetic value. The more peaking power produced, the greater the drawdown, and the less pleasing the site. Peaking power still has a market price, but how is esthetic quality to be valued? In some places, people do pay admission charges for access to beautiful views, but that hardly tells us anything about peoples' willingness to pay for different degrees of water level stability at this site. Some method of gaining information other than through markets must be used. Perhaps public hearings could uncover peoples' feelings about how much power should be sacrificed to upgrade' the esthetic features of the reservoir, but the results of the public hearings are likely to depend on who turns out and on the financing scheme for determining who pays the costs attributable to esthetic enhancement.

The question posed above concerning the valuations to be placed by society on different designs is a profoundly difficult one to answer whenever the project's impacts are not adequately represented by existing market prices of measurable inputs and outputs. In general we are asking how to discern the 'social welfare function,' one contour of which is shown as the curve *W* in Figure 1. Such a

welfare function would weight all the impacts by their social importance and would yield an overall measure of a project's net impact on society. This book offers some practical suggestions for
situations that frequently face the public water manager, but the
general question must be left unanswered.

It should also be made quite clear at this point that the methods
of analysis to be discussed not only are applicable to 'brick and
mortar' projects but also are equally applicable to the design and
ranking of nonstructural alternatives or components of a water management program, such as floodplain zoning, the establishment of
early warning systems, and the setting of water quality standards.

Distribution of Project Benefits and Costs among Different Groups

The brief discussion above of scarcity and the making of socially
optimal decisions (in the form of project designs) was cast in terms
of getting the greatest project benefits from a given construction
budget. An extremely important part of the economic problem concerns who gets those benefits and who pays the costs. There are
three main reasons why the water manager should be interested in
these questions. First, society, partly through government at different levels, takes an interest in the distribution of economic
welfare among different groups of persons. Concern over poverty and
a willingness to tax incomes at progressive rates are sufficient
evidence of this point. Some water projects have been built as
much to change the distribution of economic welfare as to increase
aggregate economic welfare. The water projects of the Appalachian
Commission are evidence of this perspective.

Second, even when a project is designed without any overt intent
to affect the distribution of economic well-being among groups, the
project and its methods of financing nonetheless always have some
impact on this distribution as well as on the overall magnitude of
economic well-being. Since society (or the relevant subgroups affected by the decision) generally does have preferences regarding
the distribution of benefits and costs, the project's distributional

implications should be spelled out, although doing so will generally
be a complicated task.

Third, the kinds of support and opposition that the water manager
can expect for particular projects will depend very heavily on who
gets the benefits and who bears the costs. Federal navigation or
hydropower projects elicit in a very predictable way the backing of
some groups and the opposition of others, not only on the basis of
the perceived magnitudes of overall benefits and costs but also very
much on the basis of who receives the benefits and who pays the
costs.

Thus the water manager must be and should be alert to the implications of project selection or design for the distribution of economic well-being among groups, as well as for the overall magnitude
of economic well-being generated.

Relevance and Irrelevance of Financing Arrangements

It should be clear by now that benefits are not synonomous with
monetary revenues and that costs are not to be equated with cash
outflows alone. We are interested in benefits and costs accruing
from projects, whatever their form and to whomsoever they accrue.
Some of the most beneficial projects may result in no cash inflows
at all (say, a village water supply program in an underdeveloped
area), and some very inexpensive projects (say, a small diversion
dam) may be very costly if they have extensive deleterious effects
downstream (e.g., ecological damage or the failure of valuable crops
dependent on the water). Thus economic analysis is concerned with
much more than money inflows and outflows.

Yet financial arrangements cannot be ignored for several reasons.
First, all levels of government and government agencies face monetary budget constraints. The government may be required to balance
the budget, or revenues from existing projects may be an important
source of funds for new undertakings. Second, the way in which project costs are carried by project users (user costs, prices of the
product or service, and so on) will determine the amount of the project output they demand. This amount in turn will affect the

planned size and timing of the project. Third, as mentioned in the preceding section, who benefits and who loses from a project are determined in a major way by the particular financial arrangements.

This book is primarily concerned with the relationship of overall benefits and costs (i.e., with the broad economic optimality and feasibility of projects) rather than with the question of financial feasibility, Can the project pay for itself? Yet financial arrangements must be brought into the discussion.

With-Without Criterion: The Basic Reference Point

The objective of analyzing a prospective project should be to assess just what the state of the nation (or other relevant subdivision) will be with the project (i.e., if it is built and operated) as contrasted with what the state of the nation will be without the project. Clearly such an analysis covers more than just the directly measurable economic impacts. It should include an analysis of social impacts (e.g., who gets displaced by the project, the effect on family life, the stimulus provided for urban migration, and so on) and esthetic impacts (e.g., what the project does to enhance or degrade the environment) for which no monetary values can be assigned.

When confusion sets in regarding what is to be included as benefit or cost, this with-without guideline is very helpful. One must realize that this guideline is not the same as looking at the state of the nation before and after the project. Before the project, certain trends of change will exist, say, a growth in agriculture yields. An irrigation project may permit yields to jump even more, but attributing to the project all the change in yield from before the project to what is observed after the project would clearly be erroneous since part of that change would have occurred without the project.

2 THE ACCOUNTING STANCE

Let us for the moment remove the water manager to some lofty
height from which he can survey all the benefits and costs emanating
from a proposed project. Some of the benefits accrue to persons in
the water manager's own town or country. Other benefits may be
spread throughout the state, and still others across the nation.
Similarly, costs may be absorbed partly by the direct users of the
project (e.g., irrigators, users of municipal water, and boaters on
the reservoir); by the whole taxable population of the city, county,
state, or nation; and by the parties who are injured by the project
without compensation. How much of this very complex scene should be
of interest to the water manager in assessing the worth of the
project?

Perhaps it would be considered ideal if the water manager, at
whatever level of government he stands, could take into account the
benefits and costs 'to whomsoever they accrue' (U.S. Interagency
Committee on Water Resources, 1950). Then we would be assured that
the decisions made at all levels would be in the nation's interests
and not simply in the interests of the particular locality where the
project was located.

There are at least two major problems in asking the water manager
at levels below the federal level to assume a national viewpoint.
First, to extend the search for benefits and costs to the entire nation may be very costly and time-consuming. Second, under present
arrangements the manager's incentive system orients him to his own
constituency. The construction of an Ohio River dam may provide new
employment to steel workers in Cleveland or Chicago, or the improvement in navigation may (through a very complex chain of market
transactions) result in lower electricity costs to power consumers

in Iowa and thus in greater consumption or more employment. Under conditions to be discussed later in chapter 4, these increased incomes may be countable as national economic benefits. Yet can the person assessing the worth of the dam be expected to look so far afield for the occurrence of project-related benefits and costs? An answer must be qualified. If a federal agency (e.g., the U.S. Army Corps of Engineers) is building the dam, then it should be expected to take into account these far removed impacts, even if doing so involves substantial research and the use of sophisticated methods of analysis. Federal agencies are charged with carrying out projects in the national interest unless explicitly directed otherwise by legislation, e.g., the program of the U.S. Army Corps of Engineers to promote Appalachian development.

However, if the agency involved is a local flood control district or a local water supply department, it is unrealistic to assume that it can or will adopt such a broad perspective and pay the costs of such a broad analysis. Each level of government has its own natural viewpoint (accounting stance) within which it has an interest in benefit and cost incidence. A city is concerned with benefits to and costs borne by its citizens, as is a county, state, or region. To say this is not to deny various forms of generosity or altruistic behavior that are observed, but generosity and altruistic behavior cannot and, in the author's view, should not be counted on to make local and national interests coincide.

The water manager is rewarded for serving his constituency well. If it is possible to develop projects the benefits of which accrue largely to his constituents and the costs of which are borne largely by others (say, irrigation projects with their grace periods, low interest rates, and subsidies from power sales, or harbor improvements), such projects are likely to be attractive to the manager's constituency whether or not these projects make any sense from a national viewpoint. This state of affairs is not desirable, but it is a realistic situation that must be faced. We must expect the water manager and the constituency to which he is responsible to

evaluate benefits and costs impinging on his constituency alone. If
the results are too inconsistent with broader regional or national
interests, then the rules of the game must be changed so that the
creation of external benefits and costs will be rewarded or penal-
ized within the reward structure of the local planning framework.

Olson (1969, p. 321) has stated the issue quite clearly,

> The establishment of institutional arrangements with appro-
> priate functions, sizes, and incentives is a basic step in
> implementing sound public policy. ...it is essential that
> the economic analysis of proposed public undertakings con-
> sider explicitly these institutional questions, for "if a
> particular function is assigned to the wrong type of insti-
> tution, the incentives that the relevant decision-maker fac-
> es may keep him from doing all that he could to serve the
> public, however superb his analytical apparatus might be."

There are at least three ways of reconciling the natural local
accounting stance of different levels of the planning organization.
The first way is to raise planning to higher levels that incorporate
most of the significant external effects. An example of this type
of planning is the effort that started with the Water Resources
Planning Act of 1965 to establish river basin commissions in each
major basin of the United States to coordinate and undertake water
planning and development.

A second way of making a local viewpoint consistent with the
broader public interests is to establish a system of rewards and
penalties (e.g., subsidies and taxes) that make socially attractive
projects attractive locally and socially undesirable projects undesirable locally. For example, the imposition of effluent charges
on municipal waste discharges can cause the local sewerage manager
to take into account the damages his waste load is causing downstream, even though he doesn't think of it in just those terms. He
may simply see a monetary penalty he would like to avoid if he can
do so through additional treatment. A somewhat similar effect may
be achieved through subsidizing the construction of treatment plants,
although such subsidies must be accompanied by effluent quality standards if local areas are to find treatment of sewage worthwhile.

A third often used arrangement for reconciling viewpoints is the
establishment of standards or other forms of regulation such as
those that have grown up in the water and air quality fields.

At the local level, several problems relating to the accounting
stance occur. There is the problem of defining the group whose interests are to be served by the water manager. Is this group defined in terms of their occupancy of certain lands, e.g., within the
city limits or within the limits of some larger service area? Or
should the water manager serve the interests of the present, established population? The water manager himself cannot in most cases
make this policy decision himself, but the decision is a matter of
importance since the provision of utilities and the prices charged
for these services strongly affect patterns of urban growth. Many,
if not most, urban water utilities heavily subsidize new developments by charging the developer a service fee that is far less than
the actual capital costs of providing the new service. The difference is made up from the general tax base or is loaded onto the
price of water to existing customers. Is this method in the interest of the established population? Naturally, the answer to this
question will depend on the other favorable and unfavorable impacts
that the new development will have on the community.

The water manager (public utility manager in general) should act
in the interests of the *existing* population of his area unless he
receives policy direction from his constituency to the contrary.
This point of view is the same as that taken by corporate financial
managers in deciding the merits of new investments or stock issues,
and is expressed in the question, Will the action dilute or enhance
the equity of existing stockholders? If this stockholder equity
view were taken by city managements in general, continued urban
growth might be seen in a different light.

Such a point of view is not inconsistent with the appropriately
broad inclusion of benefits and costs over time and space in assessing a project, because the existing population does have an interest in the future and in the welfare of wider areas. This

viewpoint simply requires an analysis of the distribution of project benefits and costs between the existing population and the potential new population and also requires that the population make known to the water manager their concern with future conditions and conditions outside their immediate area.

3 MULTIPLE OBJECTIVE PLANNING

Types of Benefits and Costs To Be Used in Planning

Thus far we have alluded to benefits and costs without defining them. We have intended those words to stand for all the 'goods and bads' generated by a project. This definition is indeed exactly what is meant, but it is useful to be somewhat more detailed in talking about types of benefits and costs. A useful breakdown of the types of benefits and costs might be the following: (1) benefits and costs for which market prices exist and for which these prices correctly reflect social values (e.g., nonprice-supported farm commodities and most agricultural inputs); (2) benefits and costs for which market prices exist but for which the prices fail to reflect appropriate social values (e.g., price-supported commodities like cotton and wheat, and labor inputs that would otherwise be unemployed); (3) benefits and costs for which no market prices exist but for which appropriate social values can be approximated in money terms by inferring what consumers would be willing to pay for the product or service if a market existed (e.g., local water-based recreation); and (4) benefits and costs for which it would be difficult to imagine any kind of market-like process capable of registering a meaningful monetary valuation (e.g., the creation or maintenance of a beautiful view or historic site, the maintenance of a water quality higher than that required for health or commercial reasons, and the destruction of a unique riverscape).

The theory of benefit-cost analysis has always recognized that benefits and costs of all four classes usually result from the construction and operation of a project. A good benefit-cost analysis (project appraisal) not only has always compared the monetarily measured benefits and costs, but also has described in whatever terms were feasible the nonquantifiable, noncommensurable benefits and costs.

15

When the appraisal or design of a project is based purely on benefits and costs of the first three classes above (i.e., on the aggregate of benefits and costs that are comparable in monetary terms), the
analysis is typically said to be based on the criterion of economic
efficiency. From a national accounting stance, this criterion can be
interpreted very roughly as national income maximization, though the
criterion will encompass many goods and bads that do not appear in the
national income account (see chapter 5 for details of benefit and cost
measurement).

The economic growth orientations of the post-World War II period,
following as it did a decade of depression, provided an atmosphere in
which the national economic efficiency criterion appeared to represent
the things that society appeared to be most interested in. During
this period, the emphasis of the applied benefit-cost analyses in the
water resources field was almost exclusively on those benefits and
costs that could be measured and made comparable in monetary terms and
as viewed from a national accounting stance. (The national accounting
stance is not hard to explain, since there has been relatively little
application of benefit-cost analysis by any group other than federal
agencies.) The emphasis on the monetarily measurable and comparable
goods and bads has been defended on several grounds (e.g., Freeman
and Haveman, 1970).

1. Most of the impacts of public water projects consist of mar-
ketable goods and services (electrical energy, municipal water supply,
navigation, irrigation water, and so on) that are produced in the public rather than the private sector solely because a competitive market structure cannot be maintained for the provision of these services. (The inability to maintain a competitive private market structure often occurs because of 'economies of scale,' i.e., the ability
to reduce costs as the output of the enterprise increases. This ability leads to a situation where costs will be lowest if the entire market is served by one producer. If the market is initially open to
free competitive entry, the market will come to be dominated by one
producer.

Inappropriateness of having a market supplied by private producers
can occur when the good or service is of a public good nature, i.e.,

when the use of the good or service by one person does not diminish
the amount available to others. Typical examples are national defense
and, to a lesser extent, police and fire protection. Enhancement of
the physical environment has many attributes of a public good. The
provision of public goods by private suppliers is made difficult by
the inability to charge directly for their consumption (e.g., national
defense since a person will benefit whether he pays or not) or by the
inappropriateness of charging directly for services that are not di-
minished in quantity or quality by one person's use.

Another situation in which the public sector supply may be appropriate is in the case of so-called 'merit wants,' i.e., goods or services that society has decided should be consumed in greater quantity
than would be the case in a private market situation. The main examples are education and public health measures, such as innoculations
and chest X rays. Basically, there is no reason why such goods can't
be provided by private enterprises under public subsidy so that the
price can be appropriately reduced.)

2. Other types of impacts that can be brought about by water projects, especially shifting income or income-earning capacity in favor
of particular groups and enhancing the physical environment, can be
accomplished more efficiently through other types of public and private programs, e.g., education, land use controls, industrial regulation, and so on.

3. Our ability to predict and measure other types of impacts has
been quite limited, and no methods have been evolved to make such impacts comparable even when they are physically measurable.

It is the author's personal opinion that the first two arguments
remain largely valid today. Public water projects produce mostly sal-
able goods or services that are directly valued in the marketplace
(e.g., certain irrigated crops and hydroelectric power) or that can
have their values inferred from market-generated data (e.g., municipal
water supplies, water-based recreation, and flood control). It is
true, however, that nonquantifiable, nonmarketable benefits are being
increasingly accepted by the legislatures and by the public as justification for new projects or new management policies. Prime examples
are found in the water quality area where the imposition of standards

and large expenditures on treatment plants are justified on a
nonquantified desire to clean up the environment rather than on a
demonstration that monetarily measurable benefits exceed costs.

Regarding point 2, it certainly has not been demonstrated that
water projects are particularly efficient devices for redistributing
income-earning power, e.g., Appalachia (see Howe, 1968a). Further,
the environmental effects of water storage projects appear to elicit
public wrath as frequently as public praise.

Finally, as an example of point 3, techniques for environmental
description (let alone valuation) are just in their infancy (Leopold,
1969; Leopold and Marchand, 1968). Whatever the desirability of including environmental effects as a project objective, we are technically in a poor position to do so. This statement does not imply that
environmental, esthetic, or other objectives should be omitted from
our analyses, but rather implies that a great deal of work is needed
before we can have as much confidence in the measures of these objectives as we have in economic efficiency as currently measured. In the
meantime, descriptions of environmental and other impacts must comprise a part of every project or system evaluation.

Certainly, water resource development has historically served objectives that were not stated in terms of economic efficiency, e.g.,
the opening up of the Northwest Territories through the provision of
navigable waterways, the settlement of the West through the provision
of irrigation water, and the attraction of industry and commerce
through the provision of cheap power, water supply, and waste disposal.

It also remains true that, even if the primary objective of most
water resource projects were agreed to be economic efficiency, all
projects do have other types of impacts to some extent. Some beneficiaries make permanent income gains from a project, whereas other
parties are injured by the project or have to pay through taxes more
than they gain. Environment is changed for better or worse. The project region may permanently gain a productive industry, whereas other
regions may lose either through a direct locational change of industry
or by having local industry displaced through the market.

Thus it must be recognized that impacts other than national economic efficiency effects do occur and that any social evaluation of projects (i.e., the ranking, comparison, or design of projects) must attempt to be explicit and as clear as possible in describing these impacts.

Objectives Other Than National Economic Efficiency

The reader has every right, at this point of the book, to feel somewhat (but hopefully not thoroughly) confused. We have not taken time to illustrate benefits and costs in their various forms nor to distinguish legitimate benefits and costs from phony ones. The reader is encouraged to hang on until chapter 4 when we shall bring in some hopefully enlightening examples.

Also for clarity at this point, it should be emphasized that when we speak of the objectives of planning or 'multiple objective planning,' we do not refer to the 'multiple purpose' nature of the project itself. The expression multiple purpose is traditionally used to indicate projects that produce various outputs, as a dam might provide water supply, power, and flood control. The objectives of planning refer to broader social goals that specific outputs might help attain, e.g., a larger national income (economic efficiency), a more equitable distribution of income earning capabilities, a more pleasing and healthful physical environment, and so on.

What we want to talk about in this section are the procedures for project design and selection that permit explicit consideration of objectives other than the monetarily measurable national efficiency objective.

First, what are the other objectives considered important by society? The other objectives that appear relevant for water projects and that have been most prominently mentioned in the recent literature (U.S. Water Resources Council, 1970a) are (1) the attainment of a more desirable distribution of income-earning capability among various subsets of society, (2) the enhancement of the physical environment, and (3) other impacts on human well-being. Let us consider these objectives in greater detail. (The U.S. Water Resources Council has

actually listed four objectives: (1) to enhance national economic development, (2) to enhance the quality of the environment, (3) to enhance social well-being, and (4) to enhance regional development. The
present author feels that the first objective is simply economic efficiency and that the third and the fourth are just aspects of income
distribution.)

   Distribution of income. Water projects yield benefits and generate
costs. From the viewpoint of the national economic efficiency criterion, it doesn't matter who gets the benefits or who bears the costs.
The difference between benefits and costs $B - C$ (expressed in present
value terms to be explained later) is the national economic efficiency
measure of the worth of the project.

   However, these benefits and costs accrue to particular persons or
groups, and society has an interest in who these persons or groups
are. The benefits may accrue to persons who would in the absence of
the project be unemployed, to persons (rich and poor) whose incomes
are raised because of project-created opportunities, to companies
whose incomes are increased, to the stockholders of those companies,
and even to the beneficiaries of local government programs that can be
financed by virtue of higher tax proceeds from project-induced activities.

   The costs may be borne entirely by the direct users of the project
if the prices that they pay for project outputs (water, power, and
recreation) cover the costs of the project, or the costs may be borne
partly by residents of a special assessment district or by the taxpayers of the state and nation.

   The determination of the distribution of project benefits and costs
may be very difficult, much more difficult than estimating the aggregate amounts of those benefits and costs. Let us take an example.
Consider a hypothetical navigation improvement on the Ohio River.
Suppose only two things happen: the operating costs of the barge lines
fall by $1 million annually on the present volume of traffic, and
certain commodity traffic currently carried by rail is now diverted to
the river at a real cost saving of $500,000 annually. Thus the over-
all project gross benefits come to $1.5 million annually. Assume the

cost of the project to be $5 million. This project probably looks pretty good from a national viewpoint, let us say for the moment, because less than 5 years will be required for the benefits generated to exceed the costs incurred. The present question is, Who gets the benefits and who bears the costs?

First let's look at the distribution of benefits by assuming a national accounting stance, i.e., by taking an interest in benefits wherever they accrue in the country. First, consider the barge lines. The costs on their previous volume of traffic have fallen by $1 million. If the tariffs (prices) these barge lines charged for that traffic remained constant, the entire $1 million would accrue to them. However, there is considerable competition among barge lines and between the barge industry and other modes of transport, so tariffs might be reduced by amounts equaling $800,000 on the previous traffic volume. Thus $200,000 in annual benefits is retained by the barge lines, and $800,000 is passed on to their customers in lower tariffs. This information is summarized in Table 1.

Now we consider the traffic diverted from the railroads. It is assumed that the costs of carrying the diverted traffic by barge are $4.5 million, whereas the reduction in costs to the railroads is $5 million. The barge lines are able to charge their new customers $5 million for the transport, whereas the diversion results in a reduction of $6 million in revenues for the railroads. These assumptions are summarized in Table 2. The sum of the changes in net benefits to all parties equals the national benefits of the project, a cost saving of $0.5 million/year.

Thus we can say that we have traced at least the initial distribution of the benefits among the various affected parties. What about the costs? Present policy in the United States is to make no charge for the use of inland waterways like the Ohio River. Who then pays the construction cost of $5 million? The answer must be whoever pays the costs of the programs of the U.S. Army Corps of Engineers, and this person must be the general resident of the United States who pays his federal income tax. Another relevant party is added to our distributional analysis. Again we emphasize that different groups

TABLE 1.   Initial Distribution of Net Benefits on
Previous Volume of Barge Traffic

	Distribution, $\$10^6$	
Item Changed	Barge Lines	Customers
Real costs	-1.0	...
Revenue received	-0.8	...
Transport charges	...	-0.8
Net benefits	+0.2	+0.8

TABLE 2.   Initial Distribution of Net Benefits on
Traffic Diverted from Rail

	Distribution, $\$10^6$		
Item Changed	Barge Lines	Railroads	Customers
Real costs	+4.5	-5.0	...
Revenues received	+5.0	-6.0	...
Transport charges	...	...	-1.0
Net benefits	+0.5	-1.0	+1.0

generally bear the benefits and the costs.

Is this the end of the distributional analysis? This analysis already represents more than has been done traditionally as part of benefit-cost analyses, but it doesn't yet tell the whole story. It is
likely that some part of the $1.8 million of net benefits initially
accruing to the customers of the barge lines will be passed on to
their customers. This transfer of benefits will depend mostly on the
degree of competition found in the markets in which the customers sell
their products or services. Thus the analysis could go on and on in
attempting to locate the ultimate resting place of the net benefits of
the project.

This hypothetical example serves to indicate what is meant by a
distributional analysis and to indicate a little of what is involved

in attempting such an analysis. It is clear that a good distributional analysis is much more difficult than a straight accounting of
aggregate benefits and costs, whatever the accounting stance of the
decision maker.

The particular social subgroups to be considered in a distributional analysis may be suggested in part by the nature of the project.
In the above example, barge lines, railroads, and their customers were
natural starting points. There generally are more basic categories
that will be relevant to the analysis of every project. Those categories commonly suggested are (1) regions of the nation, (2) persons
by income class, and (3) persons by age or racial group. Federal projects are sometimes overtly aimed at benefiting particular regions
even when more productive projects could be found in other locations.
This type of project represents an explicit decision by Congress to
trade off some national economic efficiency benefits for benefits to
a particular region, rather as if benefits accruing to that region
carried a premium value. The Appalachian program, which included
major water supply projects, is an example. In such a case, the dis-
tinction between benefits and costs falling within the region and
outside of it would be of great importance to decisions regarding
which projects should be undertaken.

In addition to the regional distribution of project net benefits
$(B - C)$, public policy is concerned with distribution of income-
earning capacity among income groups. Agricultural price support programs are defended on the grounds of supporting the small (low income)
farmer, though the really poor farmer seldom sees any of the benefits
in practice. In fact, the agricultural support programs represent
programs the aim of which is nearly 100% income redistribution in favor of the agricultural sector. (Another purpose of determining the
distribution of benefits and costs between the public sector and private parties will be discussed in connection with risk analysis in
chapter 5 in the section entitled Handling of Risk.)

Haveman (1965, ch. 4) has analyzed the benefit and cost data of the
projects of the U.S. Army Corps of Engineers for the period 1947-1962
and has found that the program resulted in a redistribution of

benefits toward the lower income states. This redistribution was
brought about primarily because more projects were located in those
states, whereas the general tax support for the project fell more
heavily on the higher income states. There would probably be a fairly
general consensus that this analysis represents a favorable impact of
the program. The analysis doesn't tell the whole story, however,
since it fails to indicate which income classes within the low income
states receive the benefits. It might well be that only high income
classes participated.

A scheme for reporting the distribution of project net benefits has
been suggested by Weisbrod (1968) and is shown in Table 3. The mode
used in Table 3 of presenting relevant distributional data doesn't indicate the appropriate analytical procedures for determining who gets
the benefits. Weisbrod simply assumed for purposes of illustration
that benefits accrued to groups in the same proportion as the group's
size relative to the relevant population, but, as Weisbrod recognized,
there is no justification for this assumption as a general procedure.

Freeman (1967) has carried out a type of analysis showing the distribution of benefits from six federal reclamation projects by the
size of the farm. The analysis indicated that on the average the projects were redistributing income from higher income taxpayers to lower
income farmers. The analysis then went on to indicate a scheme by
which the redistribution effects might explicitly be incorporated into
the usual benefit-cost analysis.

James (1968) has indicated how the income redistributive effects of
a multiple purpose project might be calculated. For the Dewey Reservoir in the Appalachians of eastern Kentucky, his analysis showed that
flood control net benefits accrued primarily to the middle income
group. Lower income groups had too little tangible property to benefit much, and the wealthy paid sufficiently high taxes to more than
offset the benefits received. Recreation benefits were found to
accrue largely to low income groups in this case.

The above examples again serve to illustrate what is meant by the
income redistributive effects of water projects and to suggest how
these effects might be presented as part of a project evaluation.

TABLE 3. Annual Recreational Benefits, Beaver Creek State Park, Ohio, Project, by Age, Income, Region, and Color of Beneficiary

Region and Age	Income $0-$2,999		Income $3,000 and Over		Total
	White	Nonwhite	White	Nonwhite	
North					
0-18 years	$19,800	$2,400	$59,400	$3,100	$ 84,800(39%)
19-64 years	27,300	3,100	81,800	4,000	116,200(53%)
65 years and over	4,100	300	12,300	400	17,100(8%)
South					
0-18 years	...	...	...	...	...
19-64 years	...	...	...	...	...
65 years and over	...	...	...	...	...
West					
0-18 years	...	...	...	...	...
19-64 years	...	...	...	...	...
65 years and over	...	...	...	...	...
Total	$51,200	$5,800	$153,500	$7,500	$219,000
Percentage of total	24	3	70	3	100

Table is adapted from Weisbrod (1968).

What has not been made clear is how the dollars of benefits and costs accruing to different groups should be weighted in evaluating a project. Instead of simply counting up the total dollars of benefits and costs regardless of the parties to whom these benefits and costs accrue, direct incorporation of society's feelings regarding income distribution could be accomplished by weighting the dollars of benefits and costs according to groups to whom these benefits and costs accrue. Different systems of weights have been suggested (Haveman, 1965; Freeman, 1967; Weisbrod, 1968), but the issue has never been addressed in public or congressional debate, so any particular assignment of weights would be arbitrary. (One reason that congressional debate on this topic has been limited is the lack of information on noneconomic efficiency impacts of projects.)

If weights cannot be assigned to the benefits and costs accruing to different groups, distributional impacts could be taken into account in the form of constraints on the project design and on the project selection. For example, minimum proportions of total project net

benefits accruing to lower income groups or maximum proportions accruing to high income groups might be specified as necessary attributes of acceptable projects. (The same results can be gotten by the
selection of either a set of weights or a set of constraints. The
latter may be more intuitive and hence more appealing to the decision
maker.) Possible procedures for explicit incorporation in the project
design and evaluation of distributional impacts will be discussed
further in the next section.

In conclusion, the reason for considering the income redistributive
effects of water projects is that every project has a unique pattern
of the incidence of benefits and costs, and society is generally interested in that pattern as well as in the total amounts involved. It
must be emphasized again, however, that water projects are not likely
to be very efficient tools for achieving a particular redistributive
goal.

Impact of the project on the physical environment. The past decade
has seen an incredible growth of concern about the conditions of our
physical environment. The explanations for this concern are many, but
it is clear that environmental impact is something that project designers, managers, and public decision makers have to take into account.
Water projects today are generally expected by the public not to degrade the environment and are usually expected to provide some environmental enhancement. This expectation naturally opens a new area of
conflict of value judgments regarding what constitutes environmental
enhancement. The glory that one man now finds in Lake Powell stands
in contrast to the horror of another at the loss of Glen Canyon.

The incorporation of environmental impacts into project design and
evaluation would be easiest if we had just two ingredients, (1) infal-
lible indices of environmental conditions, and (2) value weights that,
when multiplied by the indices, would permit 'environmental values' to
be added in with the usual national efficiency benefits and costs.
This addition clearly is not possible at the present time. Again,
workable methods by which these impacts can be included in project
design and evaluation are discussed in the next section.

What are the major areas of environmental concern? Certainly a minimal list would include all the following:

1. water quality;
2. air quality;
3. thermal pollution;
4. preservation of natural and wilderness areas;
5. preservation of features of scientific value;
6. visual and landscape esthetics;
7. preservation of wildlife and wildlife habitat; and
8. noise pollution.

In the recent resurgence of interest in environmental problems, the water quality problems of rivers probably first came to wide public attention. The problems were caused by the rapid increase in municipal and industrial water-borne wastes, initially detergents and oxygen-depleting wastes. Concern with the eutrophication of lakes has grown rapidly. The concern started with Lake Erie but was found in nearly every locality as small residential lakes became clogged with algae blooms. Problems of reservoir stratification and the resultant low dissolved oxygen levels of releases during periods of low flow have received increasing attention. A more recent but perhaps more difficult area to deal with is that of the estuarine areas that unhappily provide both the spawning grounds for much of our valuable marine life and very attractive sites for water-using industry and, in some cases, for residential areas. The chief work on the economics of water quality is by Kneese and Bower (1968).

Air quality problems constitute a long-acknowledged problem against which some very successful campaigns were fought long before it became a popular, national issue (e.g., in Pittsburgh and London). As with water, there are many parameters of air quality. Perhaps the most significant change of the last decade has been the emergence of a set of concerns relating not to local conditions but to worldwide systems. The primary examples would be the long-term accumulation of CO_2 in the earth's atmosphere and world weather systems as carriers of long-lived pollutants to every corner of the earth, especially radioactive materials and DDT. Teller (1966, 1970) has written on the economics of air quality problems of the local variety, but little is known about the long-term implications of global conditions.

A newly emerging problem area of public concern is noise pollution. Noise is a frequently unpleasant attribute particularly of urban areas and relates most frequently to transport and construction activities. Its relationship to water projects is encountered during the construction of facilities, in connection with recreation (e.g., motor boats), and in terms of industrial activities attracted to water sites. Thus the water manager must consider noise pollution in the location of some facilities and during all construction phases.

Thermal pollution of water bodies has become a major issue in recent years and has become a severe constraint on the construction of thermal power plants. This type of pollution has become a matter of concern not only to water quality managers but to fisheries' managers, sportsmen, and marine biologists. The long-term effects of moderate temperature increases are not fully understood, but the effects can in some respects be beneficial, as in the case of reservoirs where values for swimming or waterfowl sanctuaries are enhanced.

An environmental issue striking much closer to traditional water projects is the increased public interest in preserving natural and wilderness areas. The increasing demands for recreational use of such areas are generated by more people, income, and leisure and make the traditional forms of development (e.g., dam building for water and power) increasingly expensive in terms of other uses foregone. Krutilla (1967a, b) has pointed out that the course of technological progress makes it easier to produce nearly all products except natural environment. The quantity of that resource is fixed, and our capacity for producing it cannot respond to increases in demand, except perhaps through improvements in transportation. Thus the passage of time not only increases the demand for our fixed natural areas but also simplifies the task of satisfying our other needs in ways that don't require the exploitation of remaining natural areas.

When deciding on the preservation or development of an area, the question of the value of an area in its natural state arises. This value may result from present and future recreational uses, from the esthetic and scientific desirability of preserving areas having unique

geologic or biologic features, and generally from the motive of preserving resources for the future. Procedures for calculating recreational values have reached a rather advanced state of development and
will be discussed further in chapter 4. Those values can, for the
most part, be included in the economic efficiency analysis. The preservation values of unique areas can, at best, be described in terms
of indicating the degree of uniqueness. In connection with the uniqueness of the esthetic features of rivers, indices have been developed
by Leopold (1969; Leopold and Marchand, 1968). Further development of
indices of this type of environmental conditions will aid in the
explicit consideration of nonmarket esthetic and preservation values.

A final area of environmental concern is that of fitting man's activities, including water resource developments, more consistently and
pleasingly into nature's settings. Man's structures can be planned to
maintain the pleasing features of landscapes and to be consistent with
them, but unfortunately structures more often intrude on the setting
in unpleasant ways. Litton (1970) has written about the possibility
of establishing classification schemes for landscapes that would (1)
provide inventories or landscape types so that the uniqueness of a
given scene could be determined and taken into account in the design
of developments, (2) help in identifying areas for preservation, and
(3) help in maintaining a diversity of landscapes and in preserving
natural features sufficiently to allow flexibility in future land use
patterns. Clearly, these esthetic issues are of great relevance to the
location and design of water projects.

Other impacts on human well-being. Beyond economic efficiency, income distribution, and environmental impacts, there may exist other
types of impact resulting from water projects that would be of importance to the design and evaluation of a particular project. For
example, large dams are quite fashionable in some of the lesser developed countries. These projects result in the physical displacement of
large (and always underestimated) numbers of people who must, often at
quite high (and always underestimated) cost, be resettled. Whereas
monetary resettlement costs can be estimated, there are many human

sacrifices involved in resettlement that are not reflected in money
costs (e.g., the general disruption of life and social relationships,
the loss of traditional lands of religious and ancestral value, the
inducement of conflicts between the resettled and their new neighbors,
and so on). These issues arise not only in the lesser developed countries but also in the United States where new dams are planned. Similar considerations are involved in evaluating the values of flood
control projects.

The point is that whenever important impacts are predicted to occur
and do not fit into the above categories, they should be fully described and related as clearly as possible to specific features and
magnitudes of project design.

Procedures for Incorporating Multiple Objectives in Project Design and Selection

The preceding two sections have pointed out that national economic
efficiency (or economic efficiency modified to fit the appropriate
accounting stance of the decision maker) is very likely to continue to
receive the greatest weight in water resource planning but that income distribution impacts and environmental impacts are currently considered important by society and must be taken into account in designing and selecting projects. These sections also pointed out, however,
that in the present state of the art we can't ascertain the different
weights that society wishes to attach to the benefits and costs accruing to different groups and that our ability to characterize and
value environmental impacts is even more limited. How then can these
major objectives be included in the processes of designing good or
optimum projects and in setting priorities among projects?

There appear to be two major approaches that are not necessarily
mutually exclusive: (1) maximizing national (or from the appropriate
accounting stance) economic efficiency subject to quantitative constraints on benefit and cost distribution and environmental impacts,
and (2) designing a number of alternative projects with substantially
different mixes of economic efficiency, distributional, and environmental impacts. These two steps can be combined into an effective
approach to project design as discussed below.

In the sections that follow, we will use the concept of incremental (marginal) benefits and costs. These terms simply mean the change in benefits or costs that follow from a small change in the design variable under discussion. For technological and economic reasons, it is usually reasonable to expect incremental project benefits to fall and incremental costs to rise beyond some project size.

Maximizing economic efficiency subject to constraints. First, let us discuss the problem of project design. If all project outputs were quantifiable in comparable value terms, the project capacity to produce each output (for multiple purpose projects) could be expanded until incremental benefits equaled incremental costs, a point beyond which further expansion would not be warranted. Since the values of certain project outputs (or impacts) are not quantifiable, we must determine whether there are any minimally acceptable levels of those outputs required either by law or by other expressions of public taste. These values then would constitute constraints on our design; subject to these constraints we proceed to design the project yielding the greatest net economic efficiency benefits.

Consider a hypothetical example. The development of a power site is being considered. The power would be used by a city or power grid considerably removed from the dam site and reservoir, but it is also determined that any recreational and flood control benefits would accrue to the residents of the immediate area of the site. To provide compensation to persons whose lives would be disrupted by the construction and existence of the project, the legislature or other relevant political decision making body determines that X dollars of recreational and flood control benefits (or perhaps an amount equal to $Y\%$ of power benefits) should accrue to such parties. Furthermore, the same decision making body specifies that, for esthetic reasons, the maximum allowable drawdown should be Z feet and that all timber and trash should be removed from the reservoir site to a contour K feet below mean pool level. These requirements then would constitute quantitative constraints under which the project designer would be obligated to work. He would then presumably proceed to locate the dam, determine its height, the size of the spillways, the length of the penstocks, and so on to maximize economic efficiency from the appropriate accounting stance.

This procedure through which an informed and representative decision making body constrains project design to reflect broader social objectives is highly desirable but in fact is not often followed. It is much more common for the project designer to impose such constraints and to submit them to the decision making body for approval. The important thing is the opportunity for the decision makers to review the design and some alternatives before the design becomes fixed.

The decision making body (let's call it the legislature for short) has now tried to act wisely in setting or approving constraints on some of the noneconomic efficiency impacts of the project. However, at best their information on the trade offs that are possible among those impacts and between the economic and noneconomic impacts was limited when they first considered the project. An extremely important part of the design procedure thus is to perform a sensitivity analysis with respect to the constraint parameters X, Y, Z, and K. That is, estimates should be made of how much the quantifiable economic benefits could be increased if each constraint were relaxed (one at a time) by some amount representing a reasonable change in the design constraints; then the sensitivity analysis would be extended to show the trade offs among the various constraint parameters by holding the quantifiable net economic benefits constant.

Sensitivity analyses of this type are certainly not easy, but they generate valuable information regarding the reasonableness of the initial constraint parameters. Such an investigation might show the legislature that the initial constraint on income distribution or drawdown so increased the cost of the project that net economic benefits were reduced to an unacceptable level. This constraint might then be reconsidered.

A major difficulty historically has been that government institutions and the public have not had the capability of comprehending and using the types of information generated by sensitivity analyses.

Water project designers may have to work hard not only at eliciting public or legislative feelings on the noneconomic efficiency objectives associated with a project but also at interpreting possible trade offs and results of the sensitivity analyses. Such efforts during the initial design phases may well prevent a public rejection of the project after the design is presumably finalized.

Creating alternative designs with differing weights on the several objectives. This approach is really nothing more than the preceding method with rather large steps taken in the values of the design constraints. We assume here no prior guidance from the legislature on distributional or environmental constraints. The type of project being considered is presumably capable of significant impacts on these objectives. The idea now is to come up with several designs, each representing the designer's best interpretation of a design intended to emphasize a particular objective (e.g., economic efficiency, the appropriate form of income distribution, or environmental enhancement). Naturally, most of these designs will not be optimal from the point of view of any single objective by itself. The choice among these alternative designs must be left up to the legislature although the designer will undoubtedly be expected to make a recommendation. Under present practices, the legislature is usually handed only one design for a 'go' or 'no go' vote.

Of necessity, this procedure is rather vague, for without value guidelines the designer must rely on his own experience and intuition to guide him in the right direction. A plan to enhance the environment might mean larger impoundments to one designer and more untouched river to another. The designer had better keep in touch with his public, whomever that may be.

Again, a sensitivity analysis of each major design may be called for to indicate the more localized (in terms of output mixes) trade offs available among the three major objectives.

These procedures appear workable on matters of project design. The latter procedure above is being used currently on the Susquehanna River basin study (see U.S. Army Corps of Engineers, 1965; U.S.

Department of the Army, 1966; Werner, 1968) and will be described in greater detail in chapter 7.

The problem of ranking projects (not just alternative designs for one project), as an agency has to do when operating under a budget constraint, is fairly easy if all the projects have been designed according to the first procedure above, each subject to a socially acceptable set of constraints on the noneconomic efficiency objectives. Since all projects qualify according to the constraints, they can be ranked according to the net economic efficiency benefits alone.

After particular designs are selected for various projects under this procedure, the ranking of the various projects for funding must remain a matter for the legislature. Although each project being ranked now presumably incorporates a socially optimum mix of objectives, only the legislature can assign overall weights to each project. The usual valuation problem prevents the designer from making a one-dimensional comparison of the projects.

Which procedure is best? The present author inclines toward the first because of a continuing belief that economic efficiency should receive a greater weight than other objectives in designing and ranking water projects in the United States. However, the trends in current practice (say, the interagency task force designs for the Susquehanna River) and the opinions of some eminent water engineers and administrators indicate a greater acceptance to date of the second procedure.

4 MEASUREMENT OF ECONOMIC EFFICIENCY BENEFITS AND COSTS

This chapter presents some examples of economic efficiency benefits and costs from common types of projects so that the reader can begin to pick out the appropriate measures for the accounting stance appropriate to his position. The theory of benefit and cost measurement is then presented in simple terms illustrating the use of actual and simulated market prices as benefit and cost measures, the use of 'alternative cost' as a benefit measure, the definition and handling of so-called secondary benefits and costs, and the handling of price changes over time.

Examples of Project Benefits and Costs

We first consider the more likely types of benefits and costs generated by five common types of projects: navigation, flood control, municipal water supply, water quality management, and irrigation. We approach the five types of projects first from a national accounting stance and then from a regional accounting stance to illustrate some of the differences that would be appropriate for the regional decision maker.

National Accounting Stance

Navigation. Provision of a navigable waterway is likely to be part of a multiple purpose development. From the point of view of navigation alone, the following types of benefits could accrue:

1. One benefit could be the amount of cost saved by diverting present traffic from higher cost modes of transportation to inland or coastal waterways. The costs spoken of here are the costs of the carriers, not of their customers. That is to say, one is interested in the savings of actual resources used in the act of transporting goods, not in the changes in tariffs charged the customers. (The

35

tariffs charged are, however, relevant to determining how much traffic shifts to water and to the income distributive effects of the project.)

2. Solely by its existence, the new, lower cost waterway could generate new traffic. The value of this benefit would be measured by the willingness to pay of the new water carrier customers. (The problems of measuring this willingness to pay will be discussed later in this chapter. Also see Howe et al. (1969).)

3. A navigable waterway could cause the development of businesses that would not exist anywhere in the absence of the waterway. The net incomes of these businesses would constitute a project benefit. This benefit excludes incomes of all existing businesses that simply shift location to the riverside to take advantage of water navigation.

4. Another benefit could be the value of recreation provided by the improved waterway. (Only the difference in recreation benefits between the improved and unimproved state of the river is to be counted.)

The following costs would be expected to accrue:
1. the construction of all navigation features, including channel, locks, aids to navigation, docks, and other harbor facilities;

2. the operating and maintenance costs, including lock operation and repair, traffic control, dredging, and harbor facility upkeep;

3. the construction of recreation facilities that exist only because of the navigability of the river;

4. the value of hydroelectric power, water supply, and flood control foregone by operating the system for navigation; and

5. the productivity of the land committed to the project.

Flood control. Flood control benefits generally consist of two major components: (1) the damage prevented to all the existing and future floodplain property that would exist in the absence of the flood control project, and (2) the enhanced productivity of the floodplain in terms of the higher net incomes from activities that displace older activities (e.g., income from higher valued agriculture that displaces pasture) or in terms of new occupancy that finds the floodplain profitable only because of the new degree of protection. Flood control costs would consist of (1) incremental project construction costs attributable to the flood control purpose, (2) the value of land committed exclusively to flood control structures and storage, and (3) the values of power and water supply foregone by virtue of reserving some of the storage capacity for flood storage and managing releases for this purpose.

Municipal or industrial water supply. Benefits accrue to different classes of customers: residential, commercial, public, and industrial. The benefits typically are measured by one or both of the following procedures: (1) the customers' willingness to pay for delivered water when such a measure can be deduced from market information and (2) the cost of the next best alternative source of supply for those customers (e.g., public) who would clearly be supplied by that alternative in the absence of the present project. (The use of the cost of the best alternative as a benefit measure is discussed later in this chapter.) Detailed industry studies are needed to understand the factors that determine industry demands.

Municipal supply costs for delivered water would include (1) the costs of source development including the cost of water rights, (2) the transmission and treatment costs, (3) the local distribution and storage costs (for new areas), and (4) the costs imposed on customers by occasional water shortage due to extreme conditions (e.g., drought, equipment failure) that are anticipated by management but not guarded against by the system installed. Both benefits and costs are functions of system reliability. Very useful expositions of optimum design for municipal supply systems can be found in Russell et al. (1971) and Riordan (1971a, b).

Water quality management. The benefits and costs from this complex set of activities have proven difficult to trace and account for. The difficulties are generally connected with the fact that sources of pollution are difficult to trace, the abatement costs of polluters are difficult to know, and the positive effects of improvements are difficult to locate and quantify. The benefits would fall into one or more of the following classes:

1. health improvements to parties who use the water in untreated or inadequately treated form, or who draw water from wells fed directly by infiltration of surface supplies;

2. reduced intake water treatment costs by downstream municipalities (see Frankel, 1965);

3. reduced industrial intake treatment, although dirty, low oxygen water is sometimes preferable when it is to be used only for cooling;

4. value of increased volumes of recreational use and the upgrading of types of recreational use from, say, nonwater contact to water contact sports;

5. improved (even though unquantifiable) esthetic values stemming from clearer, less discolored waters free of unsightly debris; and

6. value of useful by-products recovered from waste streams.

Water quality management costs would consist of all the following ordinary and unusual items: (1) the costs of construction, operation, and maintenance of structures such as dams, retaining ponds, and piping systems; (2) the costs of municipal and industrial abatement procedures, including traditional treatment and (for industry) basic manufacturing process changes to reduce pollution; (3) the increased air pollution stemming from the incineration of treatment plant sludges or from odors from retention ponds; and (4) the increased costs of solid waste disposal from settling ponds or treatment plant sludge. All such benefits and costs should be weighed. Another frequently mentioned form of costs is a possible loss of jobs as marginal plants are forced to close because of abatement costs. This possibility is used as a threat by industry more often than is warranted by the actual profit situation of the plant, although multiplant firms may well choose to close marginal (zero profit) operations in the face of more stringent water quality standards. A permanent loss of employment will then be a definite cost to the area surrounding the plant closure. The reader is referred to Kneese and Bower (1968) for definitive discussions of the economics of water quality management.

Irrigation. The provision of irrigation water may give rise to the following kinds of benefits: (1) the increase in value over dry farming of farm output on the irrigated land due to more intensive

cultivation, higher valued crops, and expanded acreage; and (2) the
increase in net incomes after allowing a competitive return on capital of industries either supplying, transporting, or processing the
increased agricultural production, provided these increases would not
have occurred in the absence of the irrigation. Such increased
incomes would stem from greater use of an underused plant or economies
of scale. The case of irrigation raises some difficult issues because
of the many public price support and acreage retirement programs that
tend to distort the levels of prices from what they would be in a free
market. The second benefit cited above refers to what are often
called secondary benefits that do not accrue directly in agriculture.
This issue will be discussed at greater length later in this chapter.

Irrigation project costs would consist of the following:

1. the direct project construction costs, including all canals and
ditches to the farm headgates;

2. the present value of all anticipated drainage costs, even if
drainage will not be necessary for several years;

3. the operating and maintenance costs of the system;

4. the increased on-farm production costs;

5. the loss of net incomes to agriculture and agribusiness in non-
project areas when the present project displaces them through the depression of prices or the filling of production quotas;

6. the increased costs of storage or the subsidization of shipment
overseas to handle any resulting surpluses.

Regional Accounting Stance

We now look at the same project types and the resultant benefits and
costs as they might be viewed from a regional viewpoint. The region
has not been defined, but it might be a large section consisting of
several states having common interests in a project (e.g., the Southwest having an interest in a transfer of water from the Columbia River
to the Colorado River), a river basin within which the planning of a
basin-wide project is taking place (by nonfederal agencies), or even
part of a state. In raising this different accounting stance, it is
assumed that the agency evaluating the project is a regional and

regionally financed agency and not a federal agency (whose responsibilities should require it to take a national accounting stance). The questions raised in defining an appropriate subnational accounting stance have received very little attention in the planning literature. As stated in chapter 2, we take the position that a subnational authority should evaluate projects on the basis of the costs and benefits that will accrue to the present population of the region, given not only the input and output impacts of the project but also the financing arrangements that will be applicable to the project. As stated in chapter 2, this philosophy is similar to that of the corporate finance maxim that no expenditures or financing arrangements should be undertaken if they will dilute the common stock equity. If in gross conflict with a national viewpoint, the rules of the game should be changed.

Navigation. The regional authority would count the following as benefits:

1. savings to local shippers;

2. increased profits of local barge lines or shipping companies;

3. increased net incomes of other local companies that are involved in construction or upkeep of the waterway;

4. increase in taxes levied against 'foreign owned' corporations that move into the region solely because of the navigation project;

5. increased wage and salary incomes of existing residents brought about through employment opportunities traceable to the project;

6. recreation benefits to residents and increased incomes from recreation catering to outsiders.

(In regard to point 4 mentioned above, from a national viewpoint, many taxes are treated as transfer payments (no resource cost involved) and omitted from benefit and cost calculations. However, if a state or region can recover in taxes part of the incomes that would otherwise accrue to factor owners outside the region, then the region has gained command over real resources.) It is easily seen that benefit accounting becomes conceptually more difficult at levels below the national viewpoint. As explained in chapter 2, this difficulty is to be expected since regional benefit accounting consists of a partial distributional analysis.

The costs of a federal navigation project as seen from the regional authority's point of view could consist of the following: (1) the proportion of construction and operating, maintenance, and replacement (OM and R) costs paid by the region and its occupants, perhaps approximated by the ratio of regional federal income taxes paid to total federal income taxes collected on the presently correct assumption that these costs come from the general federal tax base; (2) any local contributions required for related harbor improvement or flood control measures; and (3) nonfederal recreation costs. The point is that under present federal financing arrangements, navigation projects cost the local area very little. If local shippers or barge lines are benefited, it is thus likely that even a project having national costs far in excess of national benefits will look attractive from the local viewpoint.

Municipal water supply. From a regional or local viewpoint, the benefits probably would be precisely those indicated from a national viewpoint. However, the costs that are relevant from the more localized viewpoint will depend on the financing available for the project. For example, if the project should involve reservoir construction by the U.S. Army Corps of Engineers or the Bureau of Reclamation, their reimbursement policies would determine what costs would be borne by the local area. The federal agencies have traditionally offered more attractive financing terms than those that could be obtained by the locality itself. There may be federal subsidies for other parts of the supply system, and these subsidies again affect the portion of the real cost that falls against the local authority.

Urban storm drainage. This new project type is introduced to permit further consideration of the local accounting stance. Let us consider a municipal accounting of benefits and costs of an ingenious scheme for storm runoff control devised for Denver's commercial redevelopment projects by the firm of Wright and McLaughlin, Engineers. The basic idea was to provide for the local retention of up to 3 inches of rainfall on the roofs of buildings, on the surfaces of parking lots, and in decorative ponds in the area.

From the project builder's point of view, the benefits would be (1) the avoided costs of the traditional drainage system that he would otherwise be required to install and (2) the increased attractiveness of the overall project brought about by the avoidance of some of the traditional drainage ditches and pipes and by the presence of the ponds. (These values would be difficult to quantify but certainly would be mentioned in any project assessment.) From the local government's point of view, there would be additional real benefits, namely, the decrease in needed downstream runoff capacity, which could be avoided as a result of the local retention of storm water.

The above examples should suffice to illustrate some of the basic types of quantifiable benefits and costs generated by water projects and to illustrate some of the differences in benefit and cost accounting that stem from differing accounting viewpoints.

Measurement of Benefits and Costs Comparable in Monetary (Dollar) Terms

The primary measure of the economic accomplishments of the national economy is the gross national product (GNP), the market value of what the economy is currently producing for consumption, investment, and export purposes. The GNP is, however, a very imperfect measure of real economic welfare. A new public park gives pleasure to many people, and yet its only appearance in the GNP is through the outlay of the land purchase price and the incomes generated during the construction phase and during upkeep and maintenance. All these items are items of cost, not benefit. The continued services of the park are never reflected, not because public park services are different in principle from other goods and services, but only because accepted GNP accounting conventions fail to incorporate most imputed values. A factory whose value-added is included in the GNP may poison the air with smoke and fumes injurious to others, but no deduction from the GNP is made to reflect this adverse cost. Thus the measures of benefits and costs in a good project assessment (benefit-cost analysis) must extend beyond the market values that comprise the GNP.

Within the appropriate geographical accounting stance, the project analysis should include benefits and costs without regard to whom these benefits and costs accrue. Thus from the provision of a healthful public water supply not only will the direct users of the water benefit, but also persons coming in contact with the direct users will benefit from less exposure to disease. For another example, an irrigation project not only may yield higher incomes to the farmers but also may make it possible to employ otherwise unemployed workers in agricultural processing or transport industries. The fact that these increases in income accrue to indirect beneficiaries makes the increases no less relevant to the analysis. As an example on the cost side, if a new irrigation project would deny water to users downstream who would suffer losses of income as a result of the project, then those losses would become a cost of the project in no less a way than the cost of the irrigation works themselves.

The most explicit benefits from building a project are measured by the market values of the goods or services produced by the project. Thus an irrigation project produces rice, vegetables, or maize having a value in the market. Since there may be different prices in different markets at different times, questions may remain about which prices to use, but at least market prices are available.

The same situation is true for costs. The most explicit costs are those related to project inputs for which funds have to be paid out. In the case of irrigation, the costs of constructing the reservoir, the main canals and ditches, the costs of farm machinery, roads, fertilizers, labor, and so on all represent explicit monetary costs. Again, when the analysis is being made, there may be several prices applicable to each input depending on the place of acquisition, quality, and so on, but market prices are available.

Market price as a measure of benefits and costs. The most obvious way of assigning numerical benefits to a project is to determine the market value of the outputs it produces. Naturally, prices vary seasonally and from area to area. If prices are stable over time except for seasonal variations, a quantity-weighted average annual price would be appropriate (i.e., total sales proceeds divided by the quantity

sold). Such a price should be computed for the point of production
rather than for some distant market where the output will eventually
be sold. That is, a deduction from the ultimate market price should
be made for necessary transport costs, or the transport costs should
be included as project costs. If markets are operating smoothly, the
price differences among locations should just equal the differences in
transport costs.

If a project's output is not large relative to the total market, the
project will probably not affect market prices. Current prices may
then be used to value the output. However, if a project's output is
large relative to total current production, the appearance of that output on the market will force prices down. This depression of price
must be anticipated in the analysis of benefits. The only way of calculating this effect is to know the demand function for the commodity
in question. Such a function is shown on Figure 2.

The demand function shows the marginal valuation (value of the last
unit of output placed on the market) of the various quantities of output that might be placed on the market. Naturally the Nth unit will be
more highly valued than the $(N + 1)$st unit. Thus if we are to value
the project's output correctly (suppose the project increases total
output from Q_1 to Q_2 in Figure 2), we must sum these marginal valuations over the relevant increase in output. This sum would be the
shaded area in the figure.

It will be noted that this area can be approximated by the expression

$$\frac{P_1 + P_2}{2}(Q_2 - Q_1)$$

That is, if we value the project's output at the average of the preproject and postproject prices, we get a good approximation of the total value of that output.

In reality, demand functions are somewhat difficult to estimate, for
the demand schedule is related not only to price but also to the income
of the relevant group of buyers, the prices of substitute commodities,
and other variables. Thus, when dealing with projects that are large

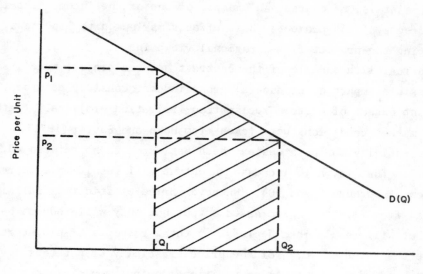

Fig. 2. Demand function for the output of a water project.

relative to the relevant market, competent economists must be involved
in the project analysis from the beginning to estimate these functions.

Commodities that are highly standardized and that enter into national and international markets, such as most nonspecialty agricultural commodities, generally have such broad markets that the additional output of a small project is unlikely to have any effect on
price. Large projects, however, are likely to lower market prices of
their outputs, especially if the commodities involved have very low
price elasticities as do many agricultural commodities. (The price
elasticity is a property of the demand function at a point and is defined as the ratio of the percentage change in quantity demanded to a
specified percentage change in price. The value of the elasticity,
which usually varies from point to point along the demand function, is
thus independent of the units in which the commodity and its price are
measured.)

The downward pressure of additional output on prices generally means
two things: (1) the benefits are less than those that would be calculated if the preproject price were used to value project output, and
(2) the producers' gross incomes may be very seriously affected. The

latter point is, of course, an example of one of the income distribution effects of the project; these effects may be quite important in
evaluating the project from a regional viewpoint.

As a real life example of the contrast between project benefits and
the possible impact on producers' gross income, consider potatoes, an
important output of western reclamation irrigation projects. (Data on
potato market conditions were taken from Howe and Easter (1971).) The
price elasticity for potatoes has been estimated to be between -0.1
and -0.2. That is, a 1% increase in output will result in a decrease
in price of between 5 and 10%. Whenever price elasticities fall in the
interval from -1.0 to 0, increased output not only will reduce the
price but will result in a decrease in total receipts of producers. If
we take the value of -0.2 for the price elasticity of potatoes, every 1
million hundred weight (cwt) of additional output would cause price to
fall by $0.04/cwt under the 1965 conditions.

During 1964-1965, national Irish potato production increased by
about 47.5 million cwt, from 221.9 million cwt to 269.4 million cwt.
Total farm receipts from potatoes fell by $173 million as the average
farm price fell from about $7.13/cwt to about $5.23/cwt (Figure 3).
The national economic efficiency benefits are represented by the area
under the demand curve between Q_1 and Q_2 and measure approximately
$294 million. Thus gross economic benefits (before deducting produc-
tion costs) were large, whereas the observed market value of total output fell by $173 million! Net farm incomes fell even more because of
the production costs of the new potatoes. The distributional implications of the expansion of production (part of which resulted from a
large expansion of reclamation-served irrigation) were clearly pro-
found, for the benefits transferred to potato buyers not only con-
sisted of the national efficiency benefits of the acreage expansion but
also included the transfer of at least $173 million from producers to
users in the form of lower prices on all output.

Perhaps the reader can see that the appropriate use of market prices
for benefit measurement involves some subtleties of a nontrivial nature.
It is still true, however, that market prices and empirically estimated
demand functions are our primary source of information regarding

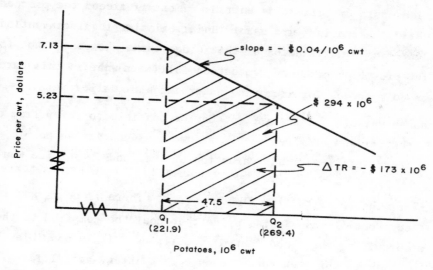

Fig. 3. Impact of increased potato production on economic benefits and producer income (1964-1965).

quantifiable benefits. Demand functions can be derived for water itself. This derivation is usually done through a linear programing model in which the water constraint is progressively relaxed (see Moore and Hedges, 1963).

Simulation of Market Prices

Market prices and demand functions indicate what people are willing to pay for commodities or services, and we take that willingness to pay as a measure of social value or benefit. However, markets in the usual sense do not exist for some commodities or services even though there is no inherent reason why consumers or users couldn't express a valuation of the commodity or service in a market setting. Prime examples are recreation on public lands and waters, flood protection, and the preservation of wilderness and other natural or historic features.

The reasons that markets don't exist for the services listed above would include the following:

1. Equity considerations are a factor. Public facilities have often been held open without charge so that particular groups (presumably low income) could benefit.

2. The costs of collecting entrance fees may exceed the proceeds.

3. Private suppliers are unable under existing legal conventions to collect from beneficiaries or to exclude those who choose not to pay. The provision of flood protection falls somewhat in this category, as do measures for improving water and air quality.

Even though markets don't exist, it may be possible to infer from observed behavior and from reasonable assumptions concerning people's value systems what a rational valuation of the good or service would be.

Consider the benefits from flood control. There is no market in which flood control has a going price that could be compared to the costs of providing the flood control facilities. It is possible, however, to estimate how much annual damage to existing activities will be averted by a proposed project and to estimate the value of flood control to the new uses that will develop as a result of the project. It seems reasonable to assume that present floodplain occupants would be willing to pay any price up to the full amount of the expected damage to be avoided rather than go without the project. Estimates of the values to new uses will be more difficult to make, since the new uses are not necessarily obvious, except perhaps in the case of agriculture. We could thus attempt to calculate a willingness to pay for flood control by the potential beneficiaries. This calculation is an example of simulating the way a competitive market would determine the demand function on flood control.

Another conceptually more complex example of simulating the operation of a market is found in recently developed methods for valuing public water-based recreation opportunities. These recreation opportunities are a particularly important feature of water developments from small town reservoirs to regional water systems, especially in light of the rapidly growing demands for such activity, stimulated by greater leisure and growing incomes. A monograph by J. Knetsch in this Water Resources Monograph Series deals in detail with recreation analysis; but a brief discussion will be given here, and more detail will be given in the last chapter.

Many recreation services do have active markets; ski resorts, beach resorts, and tennis and golf clubs abound. The reasons for having to simulate the values of recreation on public water bodies are (1) that admission fees are frequently not charged and are often nominal when they exist (thus there is no market test of willingness to pay), and (2) that the value of recreation needs to be known for planning purposes before the project exists, so the planner has no opportunity to observe how people respond to prices, if charged, or even to survey people to ask questions. We thus need methods that are capable of estimating willingness to pay and that are transferable among project types so that these methods can be used in planning.

Clawson and Knetsch (1966), generalizing on the earlier conceptual work of Hotelling, developed a method by which travel costs are used as surrogates for recreationists' willingness to pay for the use of recreation areas. Cesario and Knetsch (1970) have generalized this method to include travel time as a further differentiating surrogate for willingness to pay. The basic idea is to assume that people who live X miles from a reservoir recreation site and who face certain time and travel costs in getting to the site would use the site just as frequently as people $X + h$ miles from the site when faced with an admission fee to the site equal to the additional time and travel costs associated with the distance h. From this assumption and observations regarding the frequency of use of different groups, one can deduce a demand function for the site. In the procedure, allowances are made for differences in income of the groups of users and for differences in alternative recreational opportunities. Insofar as new sites are located in areas similar to those from which the estimating data were taken, these estimated demand functions can be used to estimate both the rates of use of prospective sites and the value of a new site as a recreational asset.

The Texas Water Development Board has used this technique to evaluate the recreational values of reservoir sites that were being considered for inclusion in the Texas Water Plan. To illustrate, their analysis started with the following participation rate function (Grubb and Goodwin, 1968):

$$\log_e Z = -8.60 + 0.57 \log_e X_1 - 1.19 \log_e X_2$$

$$+0.75 \log_e X_3 - 0.33 \log_e X_4 + 0.21 \log_e X_5$$

where

Z,   the number of visitor days per year from a particular county to a particular reservoir (approximately);

X_1,   population of the county of origin;

X_2,   the round trip cost from the county of origin;

X_3,   per capita income in the county of origin;

X_4,   a 'gravity' variable to reflect the offsetting attractions of other available lakes;

X_5,   size of the surface area of the conservation pool of the lake.

The above function was statistically fitted from actual observations on the uses of Texas lakes. This participation function is then used to estimate the demand function for new sites by inserting values of the variables for the counties surrounding the new site and by a sequence of additions to the travel cost variable that represents a sequence of increasing admission charges. Adding the participation rates over all counties for each hypothetical admission rate ($0, 1, ...) will yield points on the demand function, which is illustrated in Figure 4. The approximate area under the curve up to the rate of visitation consistent with the intended admission charge is the measure of recreation benefits yielded annually by the lake.

This procedure is clearly a complicated one, but very similar procedures are being widely used today to estimate and forecast participation rates and values of benefits from various types of outdoor recreation: salmon and steelhead fishing (Brown, 1964); various types of outdoor recreation in New York state (Kalter and Gosse, 1969); big game hunting (Davis, 1963, 1964); and activities relating to recreation stemming from improved water quality (Davidson et al., 1966). This and similar techniques thus warrant study by public planners.

Concept and Measurement of Costs

Much of what has been said regarding benefits also applies to costs. Certainly all our discussion of the appropriateness of market prices as measures of the social value of project outputs is equally

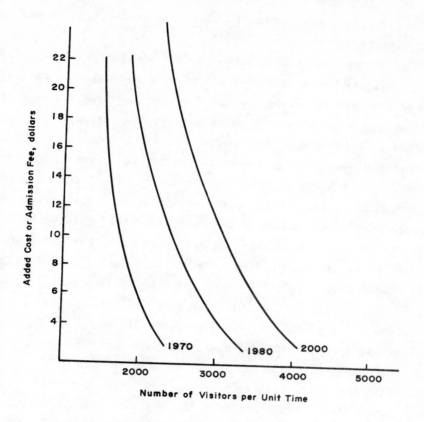

Fig. 4.　Shifting recreation demand curves.

applicable to valuing project inputs and other costs imposed on society by a water project.

The main point of this brief section is to reiterate the real definition of cost: the cost of some particular commitment of resources consists of the benefits given up in the most productive alternative use of those resources. This definition calls our attention to the wider meaning of cost, i.e., that cost may well encompass more than just dollar outflow. There are many occasions when we commit resources that require no dollar outlay but that do force society to give up other benefits. One of the most frequently observed examples is the commitment of public lands to reservoir storage. If the project is federal and the lands to be inundated are federally owned, no project cost is counted for the land under current practice. Indeed, benefits may be counted from lumber cleared from the reservoir area, even though the act represents the permanent destruction of lumber-growing capacity of the area!

Such practices are clearly nonsense, for the land to be inundated probably not only produced timber and perhaps minerals but may well have been valuable wintering grounds for game and thus may have supported hunting or conservation activities in the region.

Changes in water use patterns often involve costs not reflected in money outflows. Suppose agreement is reached on a plan to divert water from the Columbia River to the Colorado basin. It is common knowledge that approximately 150 million acre-feet of freshwater flows into the ocean each year at the mouth of the Columbia. Yet, this water is not unused. By the time it reaches the sea, this water has generated power several times, supported fish life, diluted municipal and industrial wastes, transported cargo, been used for city water supply and returned as waste, and irrigated crops and reappeared as return flow. Even the water in the estuary supports valuable fisheries and a complex, unique ecological system. Any diversion will require foregoing some of these values, the amount depending on the point of diversion.

Naturally, what the planner counts as cost depends on his accounting stance. Should the water planner in the Southwest be concerned with the opportunity costs of water transferred from the Columbia River? If that planner is with a federal agency, the answer, it seems to this author, is definitely yes; he has an obligation to count all costs. If he is a state planner, or if he is an employee of the Colorado River Board of California or the Colorado River Association, it seems a bit unreal to expect him to take such costs into account unless the market or political arrangements force him to do so, even though ideally he might consider such costs.

Thus again, from subnational accounting stances, real costs may fail to be counted when institutional arrangements permit apparently costless resource transfers to take place (e.g., the U.S. Forest Service permitting without charge a city to build a reservoir on federal land). In such cases, the rules of the game need to be changed, all real costs should be completed and passed on to the relevant decision maker through more realistic cost-sharing arrangements.

Appropriateness of Existing Market Prices as Measures
of Benefits and Costs

It was mentioned earlier that there are circumstances when existing market prices cannot be taken as measures of the value of project output or the costs of project inputs. One such circumstance occurs when the project output (or input) is so large that the project itself causes prices to change. Appropriate analysis of this situation was discussed above in this chapter in the section on the measurement of benefits and costs.

A second set of circumstances impairing the validity of market prices occurs when there are important 'market imperfections,' or substantial underemployment of labor and production capacity. The usefulness of prices as guidelines is predicated on (1) a high degree of competitiveness in the economy to insure that prices are not just arbitrarily set but relate closely to costs; (2) a high degree of use of the economy's labor resources and productive capacity so that the money wages employers must pay and the rates of return to capital expected by management reflect real 'opportunity costs'; and (3) the absence of external benefits and costs. The first point is self-explanatory, but the second may require further explanations. As this book is being written, there is substantial unemployment of labor of all grades, from the unskilled to the experienced graduate engineers. If anyone of the unemployed were given a job, the opportunity cost of that labor use would be zero since the person's alternative is to do nothing, to produce nothing, to remain unemployed. Yet no employer can hire the unemployed for a wage anywhere close to zero for various reasons: (1) the pride of the person and expectation of better conditions, (2) minimum wage laws, (3) union wage scales that don't vary with the level of unemployment, (4) the availability of unemployment benefits from government, (5) the ability to be supported by family and so on. Here then, the private cost (the required wage) of labor deviates from the social cost (or real opportunity cost) of labor. Naturally, the same circumstances may occur for underemployed factory capacity: even if the factory is currently idle, the management won't take orders at prices that yield a zero return to capital.

Cases of imperfect functioning of markets also may invalidate market prices as benefit-cost measures. Such market malfunctions may take the form of (1) domination of the market by one or a few producers who set prices arbitrarily; (2) price support programs that buy up or store production or dump it on world markets to keep domestic prices artificially high; and (3) the existence of substantial external costs (like pollution) in some lines of production so that product prices fail to reflect full social costs. Where any of these conditions exist, market prices may offer no guide to social values. Consider the old feed grain or wheat programs before acreage retirement programs managed to eliminate excess production. Grains were put into 'loan' at prices far above what users would have been willing to pay for them. The grains were simply stored where much rotted, and much of the rest was given away abroad.

What is called for in such cases? Normally, adjusted prices ('shadow prices') should be calculated to reflect real social values. Most of the time, such adjustments would be extremely difficult to calculate. Naturally, the motivation to make them is related again to the water planner's accounting stance. For example, suppose a state water planner fully recognizes that cotton prices are artificially high because of federal loan and storage programs (say, the price is about $0.33/lb of lint instead of $0.25/lb). If the planner is to evaluate a state irrigation project that will produce cotton, what prices should he use? Whereas idealistically he might reflect the national welfare by using the $0.25/lb price, he'll probably be out of a job if he fails to count the full price that will be received by his state's farmers. After all, the difference between the two prices reflects a redistribution of income from the general taxpayer to the cotton producers. If the nation (taxpayers and users of cotton) doesn't like the results, they need to change the price support program.

In the case where substantially unemployed resources will be used in the construction or operation of a project or system, an approach appropriate for public planning would be to multiply each class of costs (wages, capital goods) by one minus the probability that the inputs will be drawn from the ranks of the unemployed. A detailed procedure for using this approach is described in Haveman and Krutilla (1968).

It may be unrealistic for local and state planners who are faced with quite binding budget limitations to compute their costs in real opportunity cost terms when these are less than money costs. However, even if money budget constraints must be observed, calculations in terms of real opportunity costs will help rank projects in the appropriate order.

Handling of Price Changes over Time

Two types of price change must receive separate attention here: (1) changes in the general level of prices, and (2) changes in the price of particular project inputs or outputs relative to the general price level.

A trend (usually upward) in the general level of prices really has no effect on the economic analysis of a project with some exceptions noted below. We will be able to prove this result later in the appendix to chapter 5 after we have discussed the process of discounting future values to present values. Suffice it to say now that it is permissible to follow either of the two paths:

1. Project future benefits and costs in terms of the prices that will exist at the appropriate points in time and take into account the expected rate of inflation. The discounting process should then use a discount factor that includes a component to compensate fully for inflation.

2. Project future benefits and costs in construction period prices and make no upward adjustments for inflation. The discount factor must then not include a component for inflation. General practice is to project benefits and costs in construction period prices and to make a downward adjustment, if required, to the discount factor. This practice will be discussed at greater length in chapter 5.

Whereas general domestic inflation can be largely ignored in benefit-cost measurement, it clearly will affect the financial analysis of the project and should certainly influence repayment (pricing) policy. General domestic inflation can affect the economic assessment of a project that continues to use imports or produce exports if the rate of domestic inflation differs from the rate of inflation of relevant world prices. The discussion of the appropriate analysis of such situations is sufficiently complex to require deferral until we have completed the discussion of discounting in chapter 5 (see the appendix to chapter 5).

The other type of price change mentioned above occurs when the prices of important inputs or outputs change relative to the level of general prices. All such changes must be explicitly taken into account. For example, if we are analyzing a prospective thermoelectric project, deviations in trends in fuel cost from the general price trend must be built into the series of future costs used in the benefit-cost analysis. If the project is an irrigation project intended to produce, say, rice, deviations in trends in rice prices from general price trends must be reflected in the values of future benefits. Perhaps these deviations cannot be reflected with great precision, but an informed attempt is better than an omission of such adjustments. 'Sensitivity analyses' that show how project net benefits respond to changes in relative prices can also be useful here in determining how important such price changes are to the analysis.

Use of the Cost of the Best Alternative Project as a Measure of Benefits

There are some instances within which it becomes legitimate to use, as a measure of project benefits, the cost of the best alternative way of achieving the project goals. A common example is in the evaluation of hydroelectric power. It may be difficult to determine appropriate prices for power and energy since both may be used in a complex network serving many types of customers. It has become almost traditional to evaluate the hydroelectric output in terms of the costs of the thermal plant that would be required in the system to replace the hydroelectric plant. Naturally, the thermal plant being used in the comparison would have to be designed to do the job at minimum cost.

When does it make sense to use this alternative cost as a benefit measure? A simple example points out that it is not always appropriate. Let us assume that it is proposed to connect New York and London by a motorway. There are two alternatives: a trans-Atlantic bridge and a tunnel under the ocean. Let us further assume that the tunnel costs twice as much as the bridge. Using the cost of the alternative as a measure of the benefits of the bridge, we get a benefit-cost ratio of 2:1. It sounds like a highly worthwhile undertaking, or does it? Clearly, the whole scheme is absurd, for no one would proceed with such a costly and technically indefensible project. What's wrong?

The principal error was to assume implicitly that the decision had already been made to connect the two cities with a motorway. Clearly, if that had to be done, our analysis would have gotten us out a minimum cost. However, constraining our transport decisions to some form of motorway is patently absurd.

This points out that alternative cost can be used as a measure of benefits only if the decision has definitely been made to achieve the objective of the project by some means, regardless of cost. Then, the project under consideration is economically feasible only if project costs are less than the costs of the best alternative. Under this criterion, we can never accept any but the minimum cost way of achieving the stated goal.

It must be noted that when alternative cost is used as a benefit measure, the lifetimes of the two alternatives being compared should be approximately the same. Otherwise, we are trying to compare quite different benefit and cost streams. Thus if a hydroelectric plant will last 50 years (with certain equipment replacements) and a thermal plant will last 25 years, we want to compare the cost of the hydro plant with the cost of a sequence of two thermal plants. Naturally, appropriate allowance must be made for the different times at which expenditures take place. This allowance will be discussed in chapter 5.

The use of alternative cost as a benefit measure really results in choosing a project or design that minimizes the cost of achieving a predetermined objective, e.g., producing so much electric power. This approach to project or program optimization in which objectives are specified in quantified nonvalue (e.g., physical) terms and in which the attempt is then made to minimize the cost of achieving the specific physical objectives is called 'cost effectiveness analysis,' i.e., getting the biggest bang for the buck where bang is specified in non-value terms. This approach was first broadly practiced in the military and certainly has applications in the water field where it may be difficult to quantify certain benefits, e.g., the benefits from increased reliability, from public park and hospital use, and so on.

All cost effectiveness analysis must be extended to involve a sensitivity analysis with respect to the values of the specified objectives. That is, the analyst must compute the rates of change of the minimum achievable project cost with respect to each goal. This computation indicates the economic cost of increasing or decreasing the goals, information that is particularly valuable when the goals have been rather arbitrarily set.

Water quality standards in the United States have generally been rather arbitrarily set, and four or five parts per million of dissolved oxygen (DO) has come to be considered a desirable goal. Yet, does this goal make sense regardless of the cost of getting the DO up there? Davis (1968) has shown the sensitivity of water quality control costs for DO in the Potomac Estuary as given in Table 4. Such information greatly helps the water manager and public get some perspective on the reasonableness of preset goals.

The possibility of misapplying the alternative cost approach to benefit evaluation can easily be appreciated in the case of selecting water quality standards. If one chooses an approximately least cost way of achieving any level of the standard, the next best alternative way of achieving the standard will be certain to have a higher cost thus justifying the standard!

A very common error in the use of alternative cost in lieu of actual benefit measurement is to assign as benefits from each output of a multiple purpose reservoir the costs of a single purpose reservoir designed to provide an equivalent output. Because of economies of scale, the single purpose reservoir will always have a higher cost and hence will appear to justify the multiple purpose reservoir.

TABLE 4. Costs of Achieving
Desired Dissolved Oxygen Goal

DO,mg/1	Least Cost System,10^6	Incremental Costs,10^6
2	8	...
3	18	10
4	22	4
5	27	5

Table adapted from Davis (1968,
p. 94).

This error is often compounded if the alternative would be built by
private parties or lower levels of government that would have to pay
higher interest rates to finance the project. The cost of the alternative might be computed at 5% interest, whereas the direct project
cost would be computed at, say, 4%. Clearly, whereas some small difference might be justified in terms of risk to the investor, the differences that have frequently been used are grossly exaggerated.

Issue of Secondary Benefits and Costs

Reference has already been made to the need to count benefits and
costs without regard to whom they accrue. A project almost always will
have indirect effects on other parts of the economy. Our irrigation
project, for example, will require inputs that will have to be provided, at least in part, by domestic producers. The output of the project will require processing, transport, and storing or selling. How
much additional activity will be generated, and how much of it may we
count as project benefits?

A partial answer to this question is found in the observation that
any kind of expenditure, public or private, consumption or investment,
has secondary effects on other industries, i.e., input suppliers and
output buyers. (This is what the so-called 'input-output' model of the
U.S. economy is all about. It shows the linkage among industries by
tracing all inputs and outputs.) When the resources of the economy are
fully employed and mobile among jobs, it must be that an expanding
activity causes at least a temporary contraction in those areas from

which its labor and capital are drawn and also makes profitable the
expansion of industries supplying processed inputs or dependent on the
projects' outputs. Thus whereas a public water project is likely to
have positive secondary effects on related industries, the private
projects that are foregone or reduced in size because of the taxes
collected to finance the public project will have negative secondary
effects on their related industries. *There is no reason in a fully
employed economy to expect the positive secondary effects of the new
public project to be any greater than the negative secondary effects
of reduced private spending.* Naturally, the secondary effects of the
new project are very likely to affect different people than those involved in contractions stemming from the displaced private expenditures. Thus even when secondary benefits and costs can be ignored
from a national accounting stance they may be important from a more
local point of view.

When the conditions of full employment and mobility of labor and
capital fail to hold, however, situations may arise in which real national benefits or costs are generated in industries related to the
project. As an example of secondary benefits generated by a project,
suppose that an irrigation project produces more cotton, which in turn
requires the expansion of employment among otherwise unemployed cotton
gin and seed mill hands. Their wages, representing a real increase in
output, constitute a legitimate national benefit of the irrigation
project. In terms of the distribution of income, the reduction in
welfare payments from taxpayers to the unemployed will be relevant,
although these reductions do not represent an increase in project-
related benefits.

Now suppose that the irrigated cotton sufficiently depresses the
price of cotton that marginal farms in nonirrigated areas must shut
down. If the capital and labor resources of those areas are immobile
or are otherwise unable to secure equally remunerative jobs as they
held previously, the decreases in their incomes constitute a legitimate secondary national economic cost of the project.

The computation of secondary benefits and costs is difficult and
tedious. The concepts have often been misused and abused, usually

either by counting everything in sight as a benefit or by failing to count secondary costs. Still, this misuse does not imply that we should ignore the possible existence of secondary effects; we should recognize that secondary effects will exist only in particular circumstances and will then involve both plusses (benefits) and minuses (costs).

Managerial Analysis of a Project

The projection of project benefits implies a projection of the efficiency with which the project will be managed once the physical plant is in place. When the project will be run by competent, trained agency personnel of known reliability, a specific designed level of project output may be counted on. However, if the project is to be turned over to local authorities, the local management teams may not be up to the tasks. An appropriate project analysis must, therefore, encompass (1) realistic assumptions about the effectiveness with which the new project will be managed, and (2) a separate analysis of the benefits of committing resources to improving the competence of the management team through training programs and the hiring of more skilled professionals. These are important points to consider in municipal water plants and sewage treatment plants. In 1970, Denver was faced by a strike of water and sewerage workers at a time when the sewage treatment plant was overloaded. Professional management personnel temporarily took charge of the operations of the plant, and the plant was able to handle the overload at much higher levels of biochemical oxygen demand (BOD) removal than had been experienced before or than the plant had been designed for. Naturally this situation is not typical, but it does show the possibilities of substituting more competent operating teams for capital expenditure.

The necessity for internal controls, proper reporting, budgeting, inventory control, production scheduling and proper maintenance activities cannot be overemphasized. At the local level, failure in some of these aspects of management often causes project performance to fall seriously below design assumptions.

5 COMPARISON OF BENEFITS AND COSTS OVER TIME

Projects have a life extending over time. Generally, they yield
benefits at least intermittently over that lifetime, and usually they
incur some costs over that lifetime. If the costs per year and the
benefits per year were constant over the lifetime, to compare a
year's benefits to a year's costs would suffice to determine whether
the project was worthwhile. Presumably, if the annual benefit exceeded the annual cost, the project should be built. Such a situation is depicted by the benefit and cost lines B_1 and C_1 in Figure 5.
However, project costs and benefits are usually very unevenly distributed. Costs are heavy during an initial construction period,
then taper off to operating costs alone, and some years of increasing
maintenance costs follow. Benefits may be uniform from the beginning but usually build up to some maximum over time. Such situations
are depicted as functions B_2 and C_2 in Figure 5.

The question then is, How do we compare benefit and cost values
that are anticipated to occur at different points in time? One
scheme might simply be to add up the benefit and cost values of the
time of occurrence. Yet it requires little emphasis in a world
filled with interest rates, bond issues, loan sharks, and banks to
realize that a dollar in the hand is not the same as a dollar 1 or 10
years hence. People, corporations, and governments appear very willing to pay a premium to have money (i.e., command over resources)
available today rather than in the future.

People are willing to pay interest to expedite their acquisition
of consumer durables: homes, cars, televisions, and so on. They
frequently exhibit this preference for satisfaction today over satisfaction tomorrow, usually referred to in technical jargon as 'a
positive (rate of) time preference.' Corporations are willing to
pay interest or share profits to get money today because they have

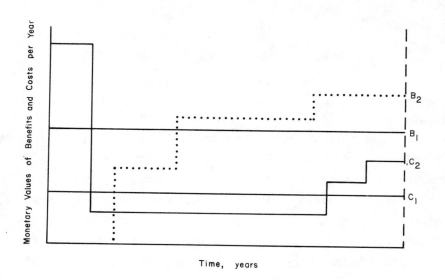

Fig. 5.   Project benefit and cost streams over time.

profit opportunities that predictedly will return more on their use of funds (resources) than what they will have to pay in interest or dividends.   State and local governments borrow to expedite consumption and capital expenditures but also to make it possible to spread the cost of common public facilities out over time.

Thus it would seem unreasonable simply to add up all the benefits and costs. All would agree that benefits or costs predicted to occur at different points of time should receive different weights before they are added, i.e., to make the benefits and costs comparable units of social value.

Generally, the relative valuation of sums available at different points in time is a matter that society or at least the public sector must decide for itself.   In other words, weights must be established that will make values at different points in time not only comparable but additive.   If d_i represents such a weight for year i, then we could add the weighted future values to get a present value equivalent:

$$PV = d_0 V_0 + d_1 V_1 + d_2 V_2 + \ldots + d_n V_n$$

where V_n is the value coming due or falling in year n.

How are the weights $d_0, \ldots, d_n$ determined? Granting that they should decrease over time and that d_0 (the weight given to immediate values) should be 1, we usually assume (generally for lack of better foresight) that the weights should decrease into the future in a geometric fashion akin to compound interest. If the rate of decrease is r, then

$$d_{n-1} = (1 + r)d_n$$
$$d_{n-2} = (1 + r)d_{n-1} = (1 + r)^2 d_n$$
$$\vdots \qquad\qquad \vdots$$
$$d_1 = (1 + r)d_2 = (1 + r)^{n-1} d_n$$
$$d_0 = (1 + r)d_1 = (1 + r)^n d_n$$

Since we have assumed that $d_0 = 1$, then $d_n = [1/(1 + r)^n]$, and from the above equations we can reason that

$$d_{n-1} = 1/(1 + r)^{n-1}$$
$$d_{n-2} = 1/(1 + r)^{n-2}$$
$$\vdots \qquad\qquad \vdots$$
$$d_1 = 1/(1 + r)$$

The parameter r is usually called the discount rate. Having transposed the problem this way we now rephrase the question, How is r to be determined? This question must be resolved by every decision making body that wants to use the benefit-cost approach to investment decisions.

Determination of the Discount Rate

There are two schools of thought, each with its own enthusiasts, on this question of how r is to be determined:

1. The parameter r should represent the pretax rate of return foregone on physical investments in the private sector when funds are transferred to the public sector to finance public activities (the opportunity cost approach).

2.   The value r is a planning parameter reflecting society's feelings about providing for the future as opposed to current consumption
(society's time preference), and r need bear no relation to the rates
of return in the private sector, interest rates, or any other measurable market phenomena.

We won't try to present all the relevant arguments for these different approaches here, for it's no comfort to the water manager or the
city council faced with budget allocation decisions to be deluged
with long lists of pros and cons (see U.S. Congress, 1968). However,
some idea of where the two concepts differ and the conditions under
which they amount to the same thing ought to be useful to the reader.

Assume that our economy was greatly simplified: that there was no
corporate income tax; that investors had perfect knowledge of investment opportunities; that consumers planned their budgets carefully
and their savings so that the future income from investing the last
dollar saved was just sufficient to offset the inconvenience of
having to wait to receive that income; and that persons, corporations,
and governments could freely borrow and lend money at one well-de-
fined interest rate. That simplification requires a lot of imagina-
tion, but let's continue for another page.

The point is that under these conditions the rate of profitability
on marginal investments in the private sector would become equated
with the rate of return needed to induce people to save. If the two
rates were not equal (say, if the rates of return on available physical investments exceeded the return needed to induce more saving),
people would save more and would pass the funds on directly or indirectly to businesses that would invest them. As the more profitable
investment opportunities were exhausted, available rates of return
would fall until it no longer paid businesses to raise more funds
from the saving public. Then the rate of return on physical investments in the private sector would equal the rate of return needed to
bring about another unit of saving; i.e., the opportunity cost of
capital funds in the private sector would be equalized with the rate
of time preference of the consumers. The two approaches listed above
would amount to the same thing.

Where does the real world stray from the idealized set of conditions stated above? The most important points of divergence are probably represented by the following real world conditions:

1. The corporate income tax rate of approximately 50% means that a company must make 20% on an investment to be able to pay the stockholder 10%. This situation tends to create a spread between the opportunity cost of capital funds in the business sector and the time preference of stock investors, although the tendency is mitigated by the possibility of bond financing, the interest on which is treated as a tax deductible expense.

2. Many consumers in the economy don't save at all and in fact pay high rates of interest on loans to expedite consumption. Clearly for these folks, available rates of return on investments aren't sufficient to offset the urge to increase present consumption. Their rate of time preference exceeds the opportunity cost of capital funds in the business sector.

There are undoubtedly other factors that prevent the equating of time preference and marginal returns to captial in the private sector. The difficulty caused by this divergence is that the achievement of an economically efficient allocation of resources over time and between public and private sectors requires that the public sector use a discount rate equal to both marginal returns in the private sector and social time preference. If the two values diverge, is it still possible to achieve such economic efficiency?

Marglin (1968) explains that when the social rate of time preference ρ differs from the marginal private sector rate of return r it is still possible to achieve an efficient allocation of resources between the public and private sectors by using ρ as a discount factor in the evaluation of public projects. The difficulty is that the private sector under such circumstances will incorrectly value capital goods from a social viewpoint, since in their discounting, the private sector will use the rate r. For example, a machine with a net yield of m dollars per year into the indefinite future would be valued at

$$K_p = \frac{m}{(1 + r)} + \frac{m}{(1 + r)^2} + \frac{m}{(1 + r)^3} + \ldots = \frac{m}{r}$$

From the point of view of the public's time preference, the machine ought to be valued at

$$K_s = \frac{m}{(1 + \rho)} + \frac{m}{(1 + \rho)^2} + \frac{m}{(1 + \rho)^3} + \ldots = \frac{m}{\rho}$$

Thus consistency requires not only using the rate of social time preference ρ as a discount factor in the evaluation of public sector projects, but also adjusting the values of all capital costs by the factor r/ρ.

The exact value of the correction factor depends on the years of life of the capital goods involved. The factor of r/ρ was derived by assuming indefinite life. The theoretically correct factor would be somewhat less than r/ρ for shorter lifetimes and actually would be

$$\frac{K_s}{K_p} = \left(\frac{r}{\rho}\right) \left[\frac{1 - \left(\frac{1}{1 + \rho}\right)^t}{1 - \left(\frac{1}{1 + r}\right)} \right]$$

In the indefinite life case, if the rate of social time preference is found to be 3%, whereas the marginal returns in the private sector are 9%, all project capital costs should be multiplied by a factor 3. *This implication of the pure social time preference approach to the selection of a discount rate is almost never acknowledged by those who advocate this approach to the selection of discount rates* (see U.S. Water Resources Council, 1970a, b, c, d). It is not at all clear that a project will present a better benefit-cost ratio by using a low discount factor ρ if capital costs are properly adjusted upward in the ratio r/ρ.

The real problem is to determine what the rate of social time preference really is. Is this problem to be handed to the planner by the legislature? Do we really feel that people are insensitive to interest rates, that their willingness to pay observable interest rates has no relevance to the determination of the appropriate discount rate?

The best resolution of this series of baffling questions yet found by this author is to take the position that no public project should be undertaken that would generate a rate of return less than the rate of return that would have been experienced on the private uses of funds that would be precluded by the financing of the public project (say, through taxes or bonds).

What are these private uses of funds precluded by the financing of public projects? Some of the funds would have found their way into private business investments. For simplicity, let us assume they would have earned a return of r_1% per year before federal taxes. Some of the funds would have been used for consumption purposes. What is meant by the rate of return on consumption? It is simply the time preference of consumers, measured by the rate of interest they are willing to pay to expedite consumption, 8%/year on a house and 12 to 18%/year on a car. Suppose these rates of interest average out to some percentage value r_2. Then if a fraction θ of federal financing comes out of private investment and if $1 - \theta$ comes out of private consumption, the weighted average rate of return foregone to finance public projects would be

$$r_w = \theta r_1 + (1 - \theta)r_2$$

Haveman (1969) found in a very detailed empirical investigation the appropriate weighted average to be about 7.3% for 1966. Because interest rates have increased since that time, a reestimate today would be higher, perhaps 10 or 11%. This estimated average is clearly higher than the one that government units have been accustomed to using in project analysis. The estimate is essentially twice what the federal water agencies will be required to use if the new standards of 5 1/2% (U.S. Water Resources Council, 1970d) are adopted.

What general principle can be handed state and local planners with regard to choosing an appropriate discount rate? The procedure for federal agencies the past several years has been to compute the average effective rate of interest on all federal securities having 15 or more years left to maturity. This procedure has led to an annually increasing discount rate that now is approximately 5% (but that would be higher were it not for a legal restriction on the amount by which it can rise in 1 year). An average effective yield on nontax free bonds provides a useful lower bound on the appropriate discount factor; i.e., the discount factor should be at least that high. (The effective rate is computed by dividing the annual interest payment per bond by the current market price of the bond. The nominal or coupon rate is just that printed on the bond.) Such yields, of course, underestimate both the pretax rates of return on business investments and the time preference rates of a large part of the consumer public.

A final question concerns municipalities or special government units whose securities are free of federal income tax. What discount rate should they use? The tax exemption on municipal bonds represents a straight transfer of income from the general federal tax-paying public to the residents of the issuing unit. Whereas from an economic efficiency viewpoint the interest rate on municipals is too low, it seems unreasonable to expect city planners to overlook this highly desirable source of subsidy. Again, an average effective yield on bonds of long maturity provides a lower bound on the appropriate rate. If the U.S. Congress feels that this subsidy results in socially inappropriate rates of municipal expenditure, the tax exemption should be rescinded.

The discount rates computed above can be referred to as 'risk free discount rates' since they are computed from the yields of securities that are nearly riskless to the holder. The section in this chapter entitled Handling of Risk treats the problems of taking risk into consideration when evaluating public investments. One approach to the problem involves changes in the discount factor.

Benefit and Cost Patterns over Time

Earlier we stated that water projects typically incur their greatest costs early in their project life and that benefits usually build up over time, possibly to some maximum relating to project capacity.

This situation is why the comparison of the present values of benefits and costs of water projects is so sensitive to the discount rate. If *PVB* and *PVC* stand for the present values of benefits and costs, respectively, then

$$PVB = B_0 + \frac{B_1}{(1 + r)} + \ldots + \frac{B_n}{(1 + r)^n}$$

$$PVC = C_0 + \frac{C_1}{(1 + r)} + \ldots + \frac{C_n}{(1 + r)^n}$$

We see that the larger benefits get more heavily discounted, whereas the larger costs, being closer in time, are less heavily discounted. Thus an increase in r nearly always reduces the criterion of economic desirability, the present value of net benefits *PVNB*:

$$PVNB = PVB - PVC$$

It is frequently stated that the later years of project life make little difference in the economic evaluation of a project because these years are so heavily discounted. This may be a frequent case, but it may not be true in some important situations.

Parker and Crutchfield (1968) have pointed out that benefits from water quality improvement may lie quite far in the future because of future population pressures and demands for water-based recreation. The same may be true for many potential recreation areas. Naturally, if project benefits grow at rates greater than the discount factor, the far future benefits may be the controlling parameters of the economic assessment of the project as illustrated algebraically below:

$$PVB = B_0 + \frac{B_0(1 + g)}{(1 + r)} + \frac{B_0(1 + g)^2}{(1 + r)^2} + \ldots + \frac{B_0(1 + g)^n}{(1 + r)^n}$$

If g exceeds r, the later years will carry the most weight. Figures 6, 7, and 8 illustrate three different benefit patterns and the corresponding percentage of discounted benefits accrued by particular times in the assumed 100-year life of the project.

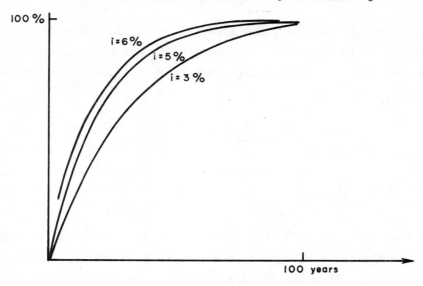

Fig. 6.   Percentage of total discounted benefits accrued up to year T over a 100-year life with constant benefits per year (adapted from Parker and Crutchfield, 1968, Figure 6).

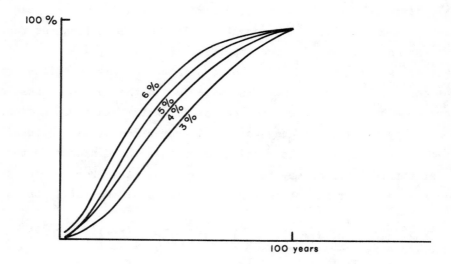

Fig. 7.   Percentage of discounted benefits to year T, benefits increasing linearly with time (adapted from Parker and Crutchfield, 1968, Figure 7).

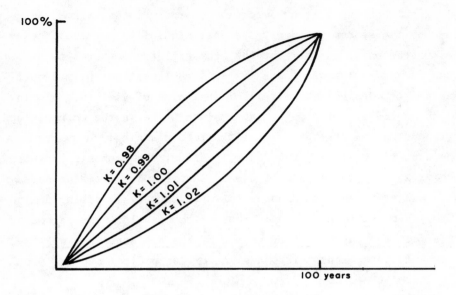

Fig. 8. Percentage of discounted benefits to year T;
$B(T) = C(1 + g)T$ where $K = (1 + g)/(1 + r)$ (adapted from
Parker and Crutchfield, 1968, Figure 8).

Handling of Risk

Projects have many uncertainties or risks attached to them: that
construction will be more difficult (or less) than projected, that
outputs will be different than projected, or that the values of inputs and outputs will differ from expectations. Some of the risks
result from engineering uncertainties, some from the probabilistic
nature of the hydrology involved, and many from the social and economic factors on which the project's real success or failure so much
depends. A recent simulation study by James et al. (1969) indicates
that the uncertainty relating to economic and demographic variables
as they help to determine the value of the project (as opposed to its
physical operation) is very important and justifies the allocation of
a larger portion of planning resources to the study and projection of
these factors.

Why should the planner take uncertainty into account? In connection with the design of water supply systems, he has always done so
and has recognized that the reliability of the system (i.e., the percentage of the time the system would actually be capable of supplying

the 'design quantity') is an important characteristic, since the
failure of the system to supply the design quantity may cause heavy
losses to the water users. But the probabilistic features of hydrology can be handled by well-established techniques that permit optimizing project design from a reliability point of view (see Fiering
and Jackson, 1971). The major uncertainties lie in the economic and
demographic parameters that are critical to planning: the population
of the area to be served, the exact location, the economic prosperity
of the area, the growth path of demand that results from these features, changes in tastes, changes in world markets affecting demand
for project outputs, and so on. Whereas changes in these parameters
won't affect the physical performance of the project, they will
greatly affect the appropriate design for the project and the project's value to society.

Uncertainty is usually a thing to be avoided. Obviously there are
circumstances in which people pay to incur uncertainty, as when they
buy a lottery ticket or scale a cliff. The avoidance of uncertainty
is certainly a more prevalent form of behavior in business and government, as when agencies take out insurance, hedge foreign exchange
commitments, pool risky investments, and so on. Reluctantly we recognize the necessary percentage chance that a dam will be topped,
that the supply will fail, or that the water quality will fail to
meet standards. It is an unhappy event when the market fails to develop as predicted and thus leaves the turbines of the hydro plant
idle or leaves a vast surplus of water supply. It may be even more
distressing when demand exceeds supply and thus causes brownouts,
brown lawns, and frayed public tempers.

Two general and rather simple steps can be taken in the general
handling of uncertainty in the planning process:

1. Face up to the uncertainty and acknowledge its presence in as
specific a way as possible (e.g., a population may range from 150,000
to 200,000 people, peak residential demands can be assumed to have a
particular probability distribution, equipment costs may range from
$A to $B, and so on).

2. Allocate planning resources to the further study of the determinants of key economic and social parameters when apparently the range of uncertainty can be significantly reduced through such study.

A frequently found example of the need to observe point 2 is the situation in which the physical features of a project will be studied in the greatest detail (e.g., the hydrology will be analyzed and refined, the operating characteristics of lock gates and chambers will be minutely studied and simulated, sedimentation and scouring will be predicted and simulated in detail), whereas only the most naive attempts will be made to study such features as the growth of demand, how the public feels about details of project design, what the impact on aesthetics will be, and so on.

Risk adjustments through the discount factor. Various steps are possible to further refine the treatment of risk in project evaluation. Thus far, risk has not been defined other than through illustration and suggestion. Let us think of the sequence of benefits and costs that will occur over time in connection with the project:

$$B_0, \ B_1, \ \ldots, \ B_T$$
$$C_0, \ C_1, \ \ldots, \ C_T$$

These benefits and costs have been treated as definite, known quantities in the analyses to date, but in fact from the planner's viewpoint they are random variables; i.e., each B_t or C_t is not known for sure but can be thought of as following some probability distribution. For example, the total benefits in the tenth year B_{10}, as seen prior to the project, cannot be pinned down to one number like $\$1.0 \times 10^6$, but these benefits may range from $\$0.7 \times 10^6$ to $\$1.5 \times 10^6$ depending on a host of influencing factors, such as population, incomes, prices of particular commodities, and so on. The best representation of our knowledge of B_{10} might be an explicit probability distribution illustrating a payoff involving risk:

Value of B_{10}, $\$10^6$	Probability of Occurence
0.7	0.1
0.9	0.2
1.1	0.3
1.3	0.3
1.5	0.1

If this distribution is the nature of B_{10}, how do we enter it into the analysis, e.g., into the calculation of a present value? One way might be to enter its expected value $E(B_{10})$, which is just a weighted average:

$$E(B_{10}) = 0.1 \times 0.7 + 0.2 \times 0.9 + 0.3 \times 1.1$$
$$+ \ 0.3 \times 1.3 + 0.1 \times 1.5$$
$$= \$1.12$$

If we can reasonably estimate the alternative values of B_{10} and the corresponding probabilities of occurrence, then this expected value becomes a definite number that can be plugged into a present value calculation. Naturally, the same could be done for all benefits B and costs C.

In transactions or decisions that involve only small values, individuals might make calculations on the basis of such expected values and ignore the possible variability of results. For fun at times, they might even choose greater variability over lesser variability for a given expected value, e.g., placing a bet or buying a lottery ticket. However, when the amounts involved are significant, most individuals prefer certainty to risk. They would attribute a present value to B_{10} of less than \$1.12 discounted by the riskless discount factor. This value suggests that the individual might evaluate a stream of random benefits as follows:

$$PVB = E(B_0) + \frac{E(B_1)}{(1 + r + \hat{r})} + \frac{E(B_2)}{(1 + r + \hat{r})^2} + \ \dots \ + \frac{E(B_T)}{(1 + r + \hat{r})^T}$$

where r represents the riskless discount rate and $\hat{r}$ represents an additional discount factor to account for what is likely to be the compounding level of variability or risk accruing in future periods (Haveman, 1965, appendix B).

Individuals avoid risk, however, not for fear of things turning out too well but for fear of things turning out too poorly. In terms of benefits and costs, this fear is one of benefits being low and/or costs being high. Whereas the calculating procedure shown above for benefits is consistent with this observation, the calculation of the present value of costs by the same method would not be, since extra heavy discounting would reduce their present value when the adjustment ought to be in the other direction. It is suggested, therefore, that the individual would evaluate a stream of random costs as follows:

$$PVC = E(C_0) + \frac{E(C_1)}{(1 + r - \hat{r})} + \frac{E(C_2)}{(1 + r - \hat{r})^2} + \ldots + \frac{E(C_T)}{(1 + r - \hat{r})^T}$$

What do these observations have to do with what a public planner ought to be doing about risk? Arrow and Lind (1970) have suggested a logical and applicable extension of Haveman's discounting procedure. They start with the following observations: (1) part of the benefits of most public sector projects are captured by the public sector through user charges; (2) the remaining benefits accrue to private parties affected by the project; (3) a large part of the costs of projects are paid by the public sector; and (4) some costs may be borne by private parties. The public sector here really means the taxpaying public of the relevant governmental unit, whereas the term private parties refers to individuals affected by the project in ways other than as general taxpayers.

Arrow and Lind have convincingly argued that project benefits and costs that accrue to the public sector are passed to the general taxpayer through the size of his tax bill. Such benefits or costs get spread over all the taxpayers so that, if the number of taxpayers is large, the element of uncertainty to each taxpayer is negligible. The present values of such benefits and costs may thus be evaluated in terms of expected values discounted by the risk free discount rate derived earlier in this chapter.

The benefits and costs that accrue to private parties still involve risk to those individuals. Since this risk is not transferred
to the public sector, such benefits and costs can be evaluated in
terms of expected values discounted by the appropriate discount factor involving a risk adjustment.

To summarize these propositions in a formula, let b represent the
proportion of annual benefits accruing to the public sector and c
represent the same regarding costs. Then the appropriate risk-
adjusted calculation of the present value of benefits and costs can
be written as follows:

$$
PVB = B_0 + \frac{bE(B_1)}{(1+r)} + \frac{bE(B_2)}{(1+r)^2} + \ldots + \frac{bE(B_T)}{(1+r)^T}
$$

$$
+ \frac{(1-b)E(B_1)}{(1+r+\hat{r})} + \frac{(1-b)E(B_2)}{(1+r+\hat{r})^2} + \ldots + \frac{(1-b)E(B_T)}{(1+r+\hat{r})^T}
$$

$$
PVC = C_0 + \frac{cE(C_1)}{(1+r)} + \frac{cE(C_2)}{(1+r)^2} + \ldots + \frac{cE(C_T)}{(1+r)^T}
$$

$$
+ \frac{(1-c)E(C_1)}{(1+r-\hat{r})} + \frac{(1-c)E(C_2)}{(1+r-\hat{r})^2} + \ldots + \frac{(1-c)E(C_T)}{(1+r-\hat{r})^T}
$$

Arrow and Lind suggest that the appropriate risk-adjusted discount
factor $(r + \hat{r})$ could be approximated by the marginal rate of return
being experienced on similar investments in the private sector. Thus
if we are considering a hydroelectric project on which private power
companies would be making, say, 8% and if we have computed $r = 5\%$,
then $\hat{r}$ would equal 3%, the risk premium on private benefits and costs
on the project.

Is it reasonable to expect a planner to carry out such wild calculations? Limitations on data and planning effort very likely will
preclude determining the probability distribution of each annual benefit and cost figure. Single estimates of the B_t and C_t figures when

honestly estimated probably can be considered as surrogates for $E(B_t)$ and $E(C_t)$. Then the above analysis can be applied.

The desirability of distinguishing between benefits and costs accruing to the public sector and private parties for purposes of risk analysis brings out another reason for carrying out a rather thorough study of the distribution of benefits and costs.

If none of the above types of analysis can be applied because of data and planning budget limitations, it is always possible to use various sensitivity analyses relating to variables or parameters of uncertain value. By sensitivity analyses we mean a study of how project net benefits vary with changes in the uncertain parameter. If project payoff turns out to be extremely sensitive to variations in a parameter, it will probably pay to make further studies of that parameter, the studies reducing the range of uncertainty. If the uncertainty cannot be resolved through further study, then the planner at least has knowledge of the range of project performance that can be expected.

Appropriate Length of the Planning Period

The discussion of discounting in the first section of this chapter indicated that values far in the future generally have small present values. This situation becomes particularly true if appropriate discount factors are chosen, since, for example, $1 received 50 years from now has a present value of $0.05 when the discount factor is 6%/year. These considerations would tend to make us rather unconcerned about projections of far future events since their present values are quite small.

Another factor that pushes us toward a shorter planning period is our inability to forecast with any great accuracy future events, such as new technologies or consumer demands and tastes. If the planner chooses to treat this uncertainty by increasing the discount factor for benefits, even less weight will be given for future events, although the opposite would happen to costs for which the risk-adjusted discount factor would be lowered.

The discussion of benefit and cost patterns over time showed, however, that in some cases of rapid demand growth, future benefits could dominate more immediate benefit and cost values. This possibility is particularly likely for pollution control measures and recreation benefits. When such situations are identified, a long planning period is called for.

What conclusions can be drawn from these contradictory influences affecting the planning period? The present author has drawn three somewhat overlapping conclusions from the above considerations and experience.

1. When one is contemplating a project with potentially irreversible consequences that could adversely affect human welfare for a very long period and when, therefore, a planning posture of caution is called for, adopt the appropriate cautious policy (or project) without trying to justify it on quantifiable benefits or costs extending extremely far into the future. Examples would be permitting projects that emit mercury residues or inundating unique and historic valleys.

2. Use as long a period as seems justified by one's ability to forecast with reasonable accuracy. This period may in some cases extend to 100 years. However, don't fudge the discount factor.

3. When irreversible effects, such as getting locked into large-scale water transfer projects or getting tied to today's hydroelectric technology, are involved in some of the alternative projects being considered, be willing to trade some net benefits as you calculate them today for flexibility. Technology doesn't stand still nor do tastes and demands. It is worth something to stay loose, i.e., to be able to respond to changed economic, social, and technological parameters.

Appendix: Impact of General Domestic Inflation on the Present Value of Net Benefits

Consider a project having an initial construction cost of C_0 and a sequence of annual benefits and costs of B_1, C_1; B_2, C_2; ...; B_n, C_n. Let us suppose that these benefits and costs have been computed in terms of construction period prices. Let $\bar{i}$ be the discount rate that would be applicable in the face of steady prices. Then the present value of net benefits is given by

$$PVNB = -C_0 + \frac{(B_1 - C_1)}{(1 + \bar{i})} + \frac{(B_2 - C_2)}{(1 + \bar{i})^2} + \ldots + \frac{(B_n - C_n)}{(1 + \bar{i})^n} \qquad \text{(A1)}$$

Now suppose that a rate of general inflation of i per year exists. Two things will happen: (1) the B_n and C_n values will increase over time above the values given in equation A1, and (2) the discount rate is likely to incorporate an inflationary premium (i.e., interest rates will increase to protect lenders from a loss of purchasing power on the funds they lend). The latter will certainly occur if the discount rate is derived from the market rates of interest. Let this discount rate be designated r. Then the present value of net benefits as calculated becomes

$$PV = -C_0 + \frac{(B_1 - C_1)(1 + i)}{(1 + r)} + \ldots + \frac{(B_n - C_n)(1 + i)^n}{(1 + r)^n} \qquad \text{(A2)}$$

Since the inflationary premium in the discount rate is such that $(1 + r) = (1 + \bar{i})(1 + i)$ when the market rates of interest fully compensate for inflation, equation A2 can be rewritten as

$$PV = -C_0 + \frac{(B_1 - C_1)(1 + i)}{(1 + \bar{i})(1 + i)} + \ldots + \frac{(B_n - C_n)(1 + i)^n}{(1 + \bar{i})^n (1 + i)^n} \qquad \text{(A3)}$$

Clearly, the inflationary terms cancel out, and we are left with the same expression as that in equation A1.

Thus we conclude that, in the case of general inflation, it makes no difference whether we use (1) benefits and costs all stated in construction period prices and a discount rate containing no inflationary premium, or (2) benefits and costs in the prices of the period in which each is incurred and a discount factor that fully compensates for the rate of inflation.

As one might suspect, however, if the domestic rates of inflation are different from those abroad, any project having imported inputs or selling its output abroad will have its present value affected by the

differential rates of inflation. Consider a project that exports its
output, and let the annual rate of increase of foreign prices be designated a and that of domestic prices be designated i. We assume
that the discount rate compensates for the domestic rate of inflation.
Then the present value of net benefits will be

$$PV = -C_0 + \frac{B_1(1 + a) - C_1(1 + i)}{(1 + \bar{i})(1 + i)} + \ldots + \frac{B_n(1 + a)^n - C_n(1 + i)^n}{(1 + \bar{i})^n(1 + i)^n}$$

(A4)

Clearly, if a is greater than i, PV will be increased relative to what
its value would be if both rates of inflation were the same. If i
exceeds a, the opposite result occurs. These results assume a constant exchange rate between domestic and foreign currency.

6 CRITERIA FOR PROJECT DESIGN AND SELECTION

This chapter is concerned with two problems: (1) to specify rules for the economic optimization of project design, and (2) to specify procedures for ranking projects in order of their economic desirability so that the greatest payoff can be achieved from the use of the water agency's budget. As the next section points out, however, even the water manager cannot confine his consideration solely to water projects, for there may be better alternative ways of achieving the same social objectives.

Consideration of a Broad Range of Alternatives

The most important single point in project planning is to consider initially the broadest possible range of alternative ways of achieving your goal. Don't be bound by traditional ways of doing things. For example, if water is to be supplied to a town, the alternatives will include surface water, groundwater from shallow wells or boreholes, construction of home cisterns for catchment of rainwater, trucking in water, and so on. A good study of the alternatives may indeed show that some agency other than your own should undertake the job. The best design work and most careful selection of projects from among the alternatives considered can still be bad planning if an imaginative range of alternatives has not been carefully considered. A very good example is provided by Davis (1968, pp. 94, 95) in connection with plans for water quality management in the Potomac Estuary. The U.S. Army Corps of Engineers had carefully designed an extensive system of mainstream and tributary reservoirs for low flow augmentation as a means of controlling water quality during low flow periods. A great deal of effort had been committed to optimizing the features of the reservoir system: locating and sizing dams, developing operating rules, and so on. Yet many alternative or complementary technologies that

might have been incorporated in the system were not considered: higher
degrees of treatment, use of high-operating/low-capital cost treatment plants, bypass piping to transport wastes to points where the assimilative capacity of the estuary is greater, in-stream reaeration,
and so on. By considering these alternatives, Davis was able to design alternative systems for meeting the dissolved oxygen (DO) targets
at costs far below the low flow augmentation costs (Table 5). Naturally, the range of alternatives to be considered tends to be restricted
by (1) the definition of responsibility or competence of the agency
within which the planner is located, and (2) the nature of the problem
that has led to the planning activity. The first point is one that
must be overcome if we are to have good public planning. If a water
agency planner is led to consider solutions to a problem and if in the
course of his investigation he concludes that schools, health programs,
or agricultural programs would be more efficient ways of solving the
problem, he ought to say so and ought to be rewarded for saying so,
even if his recommendation may mean a lower budget for his own agency.
Unfortunately, the reward structure within the public sector (at any
level) seldom operates in this way.

The nature of the problem that triggers the planning effort also
conditions the relevant range of alternatives, although not as much as
most people think. If the problem is to supply an existing or emerging
demand within an established pattern of economic growth (e.g., the provision of more residential water to a growing town in an arid area),
the range of relevant alternatives will be more limited than if the
problem is to initiate new development or to establish a new direction
of growth (e.g., to revitalize the economy of Appalachia).

The alternatives for residential water might include additional
surface development; groundwater development; desalination; importa-
tions from another basin; buying up agricultural water rights; better
system maintenance; raising the price of water to reduce existing uses;
imposing restrictions on existing water use, such as requiring the re-
circulation of cooling water; encouraging lawn and garden styles that
require little irrigation; requiring water-saving types of appliances
(toilets, washing machines, and so on) in new or renovated buildings;

TABLE 5. Costs of Alternative Systems
for Alternative Dissolved Oxygen Objectives

DO, mg/1	Low Flow System, 10^6	Least Cost Alternative System, 10^6
2	8	15
3	27	18
4	115	22
5	not feasible	27

Table adapted from Davis (1968, Table 17).

reclamation of waste water; reuse of waste water within the home; dual water systems providing both low and high quality waters; and discouraging further residential growth. The first few alternatives would always be considered; but the latter ones, which might have great merit in some situations, might be considered way out of bounds by both the public and many water managers.

For inducing economic growth in an area, the range of alternatives would naturally be much greater and would, with high probability, extend far beyond the water field itself. The enlightened water manager might find himself recommending that investments be made in nonwater projects.

It must again be emphasized that all alternatives, especially including nonstructural alternatives, must be considered if the planner's social responsibilities are to be met. A flood control plan that failed to consider flood proofing of buildings, floodplain zoning, improved warning and evacuation systems, and the possible use of flood insurance would very likely fall far short of the best possible plan. Similarly in water quality management, a fixation on water storage for low flow augmentation at the expense of reaeration, retention ponds, bypass piping, higher degrees of treatment, or even more innovative concepts such as land disposal through irrigation can only cost society vast and unnecessary commitments of money and, in the long term, the planner his reputation.

In conclusion, it seems reasonable to recommend that if the total planning effort is restricted by limited budgets, it will be better on the average to have the best type of solution than to have a finely honed version of an inappropriate solution.

Rules for Optimum Project Design

The basic criterion for selection of the optimum project design is the present value of net benefits estimated for the project. Let the benefits and costs predicted for year t be represented by B_t and C_t, respectively, and the discount rate by r; the present value of net benefits is defined as

$$PVNB = (B_0 - C_0) + \frac{(B_1 - C_1)}{(1 + r)} + \dots + \frac{(B_n - C_n)}{(1 + r)^n}$$

A preliminary investigation of the alternative ways of achieving the stated goal may, on the basis of costs or technical infeasibility, rule out all but one type of project. For example, all alternatives but groundwater might be ruled out for municipal water supply on the basis of a preliminary cost analysis. On the other hand, a preliminary investigation may leave two or more candidate types of projects in the running. The selection of the optimum type of project will then require more detailed design studies for each type of project, detailed costing, and a consideration of the different types of benefits that might be generated by the different project types.

For example, a preliminary investigation may not determine whether flood storage or levees should be used to reduce flood damage in an area. Then more detailed studies that seek to optimize the size and other design features of the two alternatives will be required before a final selection is made. The optimum design of a project usually is not judged on cost alone, but on the basis of maximizing the net benefits of all types of the project.

Single purpose structure: No staging. Here we are treating projects involving the achievement of a single goal to be accomplished through one major initial step. This step could be the building of a

structure, but it could also be the imposition of any new policy such
as flood proofing buildings or zoning the floodplain. These projects
are here assumed to be built or undertaken in one step with no possibility of later expansion. Another example might be the construction
of a dam in a valley having only one feasible site with no possibility
of raising the height of the dam at a later date. The projects
treated here are also single purpose; i.e., they are designed to
achieve only one goal: flood control, hydroelectric power, water supply, or irrigation.

The rule for this case is particularly simple. If we let $dPVC(S)$
represent the marginal or incremental present value of costs of the
structure as a function of size and $dPVB(S)$ represent the marginal
(incremental) present value of benefits from the structure as a function of size, the optimum size is determined by choosing S so that

$$dPVB(S) = dPVC(S)$$

To understand what this statement says, let us write out the present
value of benefits and costs:

$$PVB = \frac{B_1}{(1 + r)} + \frac{B_2}{(1 + r)^2} + \ldots + \frac{B_n}{(1 + r)^n}$$

$$PVC = C_0 + \frac{C_1}{(1 + r)} + \ldots + \frac{C_2}{(1 + r)^n}$$

where C_0 represents initial construction cost and C_n represents the
operation and maintenance costs during year n. The incremental present values of benefits and costs for a given increase in the size of
the project are

$$dPVB = \frac{dB_1}{(1 + r)} + \frac{dB_2}{(1 + r)^2} + \ldots + \frac{dB_n}{(1 + r)^n}$$

$$dPVC = dC_0 + \frac{dC_1}{(1 + r)} + \ldots + \frac{dC_n}{(1 + r)^n}$$

Naturally, size might have several dimensions such as the height of a dam, the acreage of an irrigation project, and the length of a penstock. The above condition would then apply to each of these dimensions.

Optimum timing of construction. A project yields benefits only insofar as it is used. Since demand for project outputs is presumably growing over time, the more a project is deferred, the more quickly it is likely to be used to capacity, and the greater the benefits generated per time period of project life will be.

Tending to offset this situation, however, is the simple fact that the present value of benefits diminishes as we push the project further into the future. Figure 9 gives a pictorial representation of the effective degree of project capacity use if the project, the life of which is L years, were to be built at two different points in time, t_0 or t_1. Thus there will be an optimum point in time to construct the project. It often pays to defer project construction. By specifying the growth in demand over time for project output and by assuming different times of construction, one can plot the present value of net benefits of the project versus the time of construction. Such a plot is given in Figure 10. If t_0 is today, then t^* represents the optimum time of construction. An analysis of this sort should be carried out for any project that will not automatically be used to capacity from the beginning.

Multipurpose structures: No staging. In many cases, incorporating several functions into one project is economical. For example, a reservoir may serve flood control, irrigation, water supply, and power needs simultaneously. Almost always, there are some economies of scale (cost savings as project size increases) that warrant multiple purpose designs if the demands for such outputs are present. Naturally, it costs something, either in construction costs or in terms of diminishing other outputs, to include more than one purpose in the project design.

The criteria for the economically optimum design of a multipurpose project represent a fairly simple extension of that set forth for the single purpose project: (1) $d\ PVB_i = d\ PVC_i$; (2) $PVB_i > PVC_i$; (3)

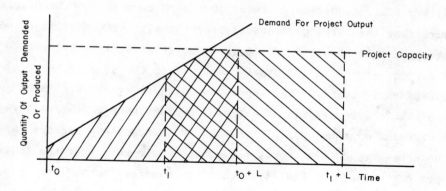

Fig. 9. The degree of capacity utilization as a function of time of project construction.

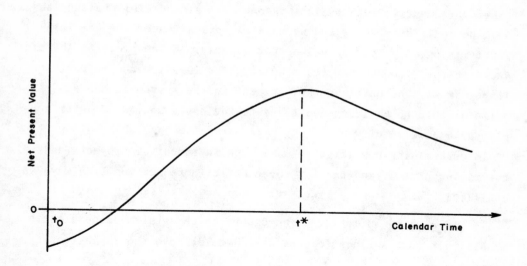

Fig. 10. Project net present value as a function of time of construction.

$PVB_t > PVC_t$; and (4) optimum timing of construction. Condition 1 means that for the ith separable purpose (i.e., a feature that can be either included or omitted at will) the dimensions of the project should be expanded until the incremental present value of benefits equals the incremental present value of costs incurred in pursuit of that purpose. Naturally, if there are hydrologic or physical limits on the size of the project, a size might have to be selected for which

$dPVB_i > dPVC_i$. Condition 2 states that a check must then be made to
be sure that the total present value of benefits from the *i*th purpose
exceeds the present value of separable costs directly attributable to
that purpose. Condition 3 states that, after the size of the project
is optimized in terms of the separable features, a check must be run
to see that the total present value of project benefits exceeds the
present value of total costs. This check is necessary because there
may be substantial joint costs not attributable to any of the individual project purposes. Finally, condition 4 refers to the timing of
construction as discussed earlier.

Optimum staging of projects. We are generally concerned with
building projects that will assist in meeting a demand that grows over
time. Frequently, each project is one of a sequence of projects that
will be built over time, and we have an option concerning how large
(in terms of, say, the annual output capacity of the project) the projects in the sequence are to be built. The larger each project, the
longer it will be until another segment to the system is needed. An
example would be building additions to the basic source of water supply for a growing city.

In determining how large to make each increment or project (and
the timing of that increment), three basic facts are nearly always in
conflict:

1. It pays to build large increments to the system because there
usually are cost savings (economies of scale) involved in increasing
project size.

2. The commitment of resources to a capacity that will not be used
for a long time is costly. It pays to defer investment as long as
possible since future costs are more heavily discounted than present
costs.

3. Maintenance of flexibility is important.

Thus a very small plant might not be optimum since small plants are
likely to be high cost plants (in terms of cost per unit of capacity);
but a huge plant, which has a low cost per unit of capacity, involves
a huge expenditure today and the carrying of substantial excess

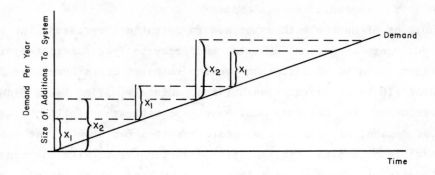

Fig. 11.   The sequencing of additions to a system.

capacity for a long time (until demand growth catches up with capacity).
The huge plant also locks us into a fixed technology for a long period
of time.

The problem can be illustrated by an inspection of Figure 11. The
size of the additions is specified as X_1 (smaller additions) or X_2
(larger additions). The growth of demand over time is shown. Thus
two larger additions would provide the required capacity for about the
same time period as three smaller additions. It has been assumed in
the illustration that no shortage is permitted to occur, a policy that
may make little sense in practice since occasional shortages during unusual drought may be much cheaper than carrying great excess capacity.
(In water systems, the concept of shortage itself involves some very
complex issues).

What is desired is the timing and sizes of additions to the system
that will meet the demands at a minimum present value of all costs.
In some problems, permitting shortages to occur but attaching a penalty to any shortage makes sense. In general, an optimum solution to
these sequencing problems is difficult to determine. (See Riordan
(1971a, b) for a particularly clear presentation of the sequencing
problem in urban water supply.) The solution to these sequencing
problems usually involves the mathematical representation of the entire sequence of costs appropriately discounted, the solution being
arrived at by methods of calculus or numerically on an electronic

computer. An example of a simplified problem and its solution is
given in the appendix to this chapter.

Short of using the methods of modern operations research, the systems designer can attempt by trial and error to find a sequence of
additions sized to minimize the present value of costs over some fairly short (10 to 20 years) time horizon. Clearly, if he is to find
that sequence, the designer must have good estimates of (1) the growth
path of demand, (2) the cost of additions as a function of the size of
the additions, and (3) the appropriate discount rate with the appropriate risk allowances. With these data at hand, approximately optimum solutions can be derived by trial and error methods.

Rules for Optimum Selection of Projects

Criteria for the optimum design of individual projects were developed in the preceding section. Following the optimum design of the
promising projects within a sector of the economy, one must choose
projects that will actually be undertaken. If there are several mutually exclusive alternatives for the accomplishment of certain objectives, the best (in some sense) must be chosen. If there are many
attractive projects but only a limited development budget, a limited
number of superior projects must be selected. The criteria discussed
below are the three most widely used and accepted.

*Selecting a set of projects to maximize the present value of net
benefits.* We have already used the concept of the present value of
net benefits in an earlier discussion, but it should be reemphasized
that this concept is the basic measure of the economic gains (or
losses) from having the project. The concept is given by

$$PVNB = B_0 - C_0 + \frac{(B_1 - C_1)}{(1 + r)} + \dots + \frac{(B_n - C_n)}{(1 + r)^n}$$

If one had an unlimited development budget, it would be desirable to
undertake all the nonmutually exclusive projects for which *PVNB* is
greater than zero, for all such projects exhibit benefits in excess of
costs, an obvious improvement in the state of affairs. We could also

say that such projects yield a rate of return greater than the discount rate. The rate of return ρ is that value of the discount factor that would make the *PVNB* equal zero.

When it happens that the budget is sufficiently limited not to permit us to undertake all the projects exhibiting a positive *PVNB*, we have a situation in which capital funds take on a premium value, because if we just had more money we could still find projects yielding a rate of return in excess of the discount rate.

In such a case, how does one select the projects to be included in the current year's construction plans? The procedure is simply to raise the discount rate being used in the *PVNB* calculations of the various projects until the set of projects remaining with *PVNB* > 0 just fits within the budget. This procedure is equivalent to finding a new discount rate that really shows the scarcity value of capital funds.

Benefit-cost ratio. Another ranking criterion frequently used to select projects is the benefit-cost ratio, or in our earlier notation *PVB/PVC*. This ratio gives a ranking usually not greatly different from the rate of return defined in the preceding section. The analyst has the option of subtracting the items of recurrent cost from the annual benefits or of including all the costs in the *PVC* terms. That is, *PVC* can be

$$PVB_1 = \frac{(B_1 - C_1)}{(1 + r)} + \frac{(B_2 - C_2)}{(1 + r)^2} + \ldots + \frac{(B_n - C_n)}{(1 + r)^n}$$

with

$$PVC_1 = C_0$$

or

$$PVB_2 = \frac{B_1}{(1 + r)} + \frac{B_2}{(1 + r)^2} + \ldots + \frac{B_n}{(1 + r)^n}$$

with

$$PVC_2 = C_0 + \frac{C_1}{(1 + r)^2} + \ldots + \frac{C_n}{(1 + r)^n}$$

The choice of whether to net recurrent costs out of the annual benefits or to include them in *PVC* will make a difference in the *B/C* ratio.
Netting out annual costs will result in a higher *B/C* ratio when the
ratio is greater than one. The comparative rating of projects may be
affected by the method used. The fact that current practice varies is
a disadvantage of the use of the *B/C* ratio criterion.

In calculating the *B/C* ratio, how does one decide how to handle the
recurrent project costs? The issue revolves around which types of
capital funds are limited. Are only the initial construction funds to
cover project construction costs, C_0 limited, or will the operating
funds to cover recurrent costs also be limited throughout the project's
life? If the former is the case, then recurrent costs may be subtract-
ed from annual benefits. If the latter is true, then the present value of all costs should be used as the denominator of the ratio.   In
each case, the proper procedure yields a ratio the value of which in
excess of 1.0 indicates the rate of return on the scarce capital inputs.

Use of Ex Post Analyses

An incredible feature of public water resource investment is that
few investigations have been carried out after-the-fact to determine
the extent to which expectations were borne out by experience. Obviously such observations would be of great value in improving the planning process and guarding the taxpayer's dollar. That such analyses
are ignored is especially curious in an economy where private sector
investments are typically put to clear-cut financial tests of the
correctness of their plans.

Perhaps these omissions have been more important at the federal
level where projects have multiple outputs maturing over long time
periods than at the local level where a shortage of water or inadequate sewage treatment would immediately come to the public's attention. (However, uneconomic overdesign of water projects is less

likely to come to the public attention and may be labeled foresight by the planners themselves). Nonetheless, regular ex post analyses not only of the technical performance of the project but of the actual benefits being generated should be a part of the continuing planning procedure. The benefits of such analyses will be (1) improved future planning and (2) the establishment of more clear-cut accountability to the public. (See Haveman (1971) for methodology of ex post analyses of water resource projects, especially at the federal level.)

Role of Pricing

The particular scheme of charges made against the customer (which we refer to collectively as 'pricing' whenever the charges are related to the quantity of the service or output used) is an extremely important aspect of water management. The pricing scheme will substantially affect the total quantities of water used, the temporal pattern of water use, the distribution of net benefits from provision of water or other outputs, the demands for different water qualities, and the financial receipts of the water agency. The major purposes to be accomplished through pricing are (1) to see that available water services get allocated to the highest value uses; (2) to adjust the quantity demanded by customers to the economically efficient quantity, i.e., the quantity for which incremental cost just equals the customer's valuation of the last unit used; (3) to provide the proper inducement to system customers to seek the socially least cost solution to their particular problems; and (4) to recover some portion of the costs of providing the water-related services.

It is generally felt, as a matter of social equity, that the persons who benefit from public programs should pay their costs. Naturally, this obligation wouldn't apply to programs the primary aim of which is the redistribution of income-producing capability, but water resource developments are not particularly efficient ways of redistributing in favor of those groups that need to be helped.

Placing a price on water guarantees that only those who value additional water in excess of the price will use it, whereas those to whom it is of lower value will conserve its use. If other means of rationing the available quantity are used, it could very well be that persons to whom additional water has very low value would be granted the available water and would commit it to uses of very low value. This situation is precisely what happens to large quantities of irrigation water.

A similar argument can be made with respect to placing a price or tax on the discharges of pollutants to streams. These prices are referred to as 'effluent charges,' and they have the effect of discouraging the discharge of pollutants the abatement of which would cost the discharger less than the level of the charge. Thus only those waste dischargers who value the assimilative capabilities of the stream at higher values than the effluent charge will use the stream.

Appropriate prices must be related to appropriate measures of cost. The cost concepts used in economic theory are sufficiently simple that fitting the many relevant categories of water-related costs into the usual cost and pricing analysis becomes difficult. In the usual water supply case, there are source costs; transmission costs; treatment, local distribution, and storage costs. Further, there are some costs related just to the heavy peak demands placed on water supply systems. Sometimes one component of the system will have excess capacity; at another time some other component will have excess capacity. There are also economies of scale in most components of water supply systems that cause costs to depend on the sizes of system additions and their intensity of use.

These are all reasons why it is difficult to be very precise in specifying just how water supply and other services should be priced. The major point to be remembered, however, is that the method of pricing will affect the quantity demanded and this quantity should influence the design of additions to the supply system. Detailed evidence on how demand will respond to pricing can be found in Hanke (1970), Howe and Linaweaver (1967), and Howe (1968b).

A second point to be remembered is that the costs of new source development are going up everywhere, not just in arid areas, quite aside from inflation. The more any customer uses, the sooner the supply system will be forced to tap new, higher cost sources. Thus the only sensible pattern of variable charges (sometimes called commodity charges) to levy against the customer is one that increases with the quantity used each billing period. This pattern of charges is contrary to many existing (decreasing block rate) pricing patterns and public attitudes but is strongly called for by the increasing scarcity of water of good quality.

A third point to be remembered in connection with pricing is that the existence of strong peak demands, both seasonal and daily, means that a large part of the local distribution and storage capacity stands idle a good bit of the time. The costs of this capacity are appropriately covered by minimum charges, front-footage charges, or other charges not related to the total quantity used but correlated with the magnitude of the peak demand. An even more desirable method of relating this readiness to serve peak demands to the pricing of water would be to have a peak period pricing scheme that would charge peak users more than it would charge off-peak users. Such schemes are widely used in pricing a range of items from industrial electric power to restaurant meals. A great deal more thought deserves to be given to both seasonal and daily peak pricing methods. Seasonal differentials could easily be introduced without changes in metering, but daily peak differential charges would require a meter capable of keeping a separate record of peak hour uses. Such meters are available.

Given the very tight budgetary situation faced by municipalities today and the tightness of the bond markets, the absorption of the capital costs of new services by the residential, commercial, or industrial developers demanding the services seems quite desirable. This absorption has a two-fold beneficial effect: (1) it reduces the amounts by which established water system customers subsidize new users; and (2) it reduces the long-term burden of financing on the utility or municipality.

Placing the capital costs on the shoulders of developers of new or improved properties (often referred to as 'plant investment fees') has been objected to on the grounds that the cost would stifle development or reduce growth. This result is very unlikely, given the magnitude of the capital costs of new services. For single family residences,

the full capital costs, including the development of new source capacity, may range from $800 to $1500. From an economic viewpoint,
if payment of full costs precludes some development, the development
should not be undertaken anyway.

A frequently heard objection to pricing water appropriately high
is that higher rates will hurt the poor. Whereas the poor would, along
with everyone else, pay more if rates were raised, there must certainly be more direct and efficient ways of helping the poor than to under-
price water for all customers. Subsidized housing, better education,
special counseling programs, and so on would get to the target group
much more effectively without inducing wasteful water use practices in
all the population.

From a practical viewpoint, a highly desirable method of pricing
urban water services would involve the following cost distinctions:
(1) the capital costs of developing new supply capacity, aside from
the costs of new source development; (2) the costs of new source development; (3) the current system operating, maintenance, and replacement costs; and (4) the administrative overhead costs. The costs of
item 1, computed for reasonably-sized additions to the components of
the system would be spread over new additions to the system in the form
of plant investments fees (PIF) paid by the developer of the new or expanded services. There should be a graduation of the PIF related to
the peak demands that the particular customer will place on the system.
For residential areas, the best surrogate for peak demands is likely
to be the irrigable area of the lawn and garden. A second best measure would be the value of the residence. For commercial and industrial users, an appropriate surrogate for peak demands might be size
of service, or perhaps forecasts of peak rates of use based on actual
customer plant design.

For pricing purposes, new source development costs should be used
as the measure of source costs for *all water* provided by the system,
regardless of actual historical costs of earlier source developments.
This point is always difficult to understand, but the increasing uses
of water by established customers just as much as the arrival of new

customers force the system to acquire or develop new sources. These marginal (incremental) source development costs should be reflected in the rate schedule of all customers, new or old and regardless of whether or not the water actually comes from the new sources. Thus each customer's decision to use more water will be based on a comparison of the value of the water to him with the costs he is causing the water system to incur. (Some single purpose water districts have legal restrictions against accruing surpluses, which the above practice often would imply. As long as such a surplus can be distributed to district members in some way not related to the amount of water used, then such a distribution will not interfere with efficient water use decisions.)

Current system OM and R costs should also be recovered through the commodity charge. Finally, it is probably desirable to cover the administrative overhead costs of the system through the imposition of a fixed charge per billing period.

In summary, the pricing structure of a water supply utility should consist of (1) a plant investment fee for all new or improved services sufficient to cover all nonsource-related capital costs of providing the new services and graduated upward in relation to the peak demands to be placed on the system; (2) a structure of commodity charges for all customers sufficient to cover marginal source costs plus all OM and R costs, the structure being of an increasing block nature related to total quantity used; and (3) a fixed fee per billing period sufficient to cover administrative costs of the system.

Pricing water services to recover all costs from users has two further, indirect, but highly important functions: (1) to facilitate economically rational decision making where alternative systems must be compared and (2) to avoid the buildup of political pressure to perpetuate highly subsidized water services.

An example of the first function is found in local decisions regarding flood control. Alternatives such as flood proofing buildings, zoning, improved warning and evacuation systems, and even (in part) flood walls must be paid for by the locality. At the same time, flood control storage in federal reservoirs is provided free. Whereas some combination of these approaches might result in achieving protection for the least cost, the locality is likely to push for the program of least cost to that locality. This tendency results in too much flood storage and not enough reliance on the other alternatives.

Regarding the second point above, it is often argued (particularly by economists) that when a water utility has excess capacity, this utility might as well price water very low so that the capacity will be used more quickly and fully. The argument usually assumes that the price of water services will then be raised toward the full cost of new additions as the capacity is reached. This position on the pricing issue has serious drawbacks:

1. Generally, different parts of the system have different capacities, and these differences make the notion of excess capacity fuzzy.

2. The low pricing of water and the consequently greater demands just speed the day when added capacity will have to be built.

3. If price is kept low during a period of excess capacity, customers are likely to make long-lived decisions affecting water use based on the low price. These customers may then suffer unexpected losses when water rates are later raised. Examples would be homeowners installing large lawns and many water-using appliances, or an industry installing a water intensive production process or once-through cooling.

4. Once a low price is established, highly interested and articulate beneficiary groups will often be able to bring political pressure to bear to maintain the low price on services of existing facilities and to extend the same pricing to new facilities.

These points fortify the arguments for the pricing principles suggested above.

Appendix: A Simplified Staging Problem

Let us suppose that we are to build a water supply for a new town. We assume that the capacity of the supply system must at all times be

adequate to meet the annual demands placed on it. The following additional assumptions are made:

1. The annual demand for water starts at zero and rises at w
units per year. Thus total water demanded in year t will be $t \cdot w$.

2. All additions to the system will last indefinitely without replacement under appropriate maintenance.

3. The present value of the construction, operating, and maintenance costs of each addition can be represented by a cost function
$TC(x)$, where x represents the annual capacity of the addition.

4. All additions will be the same size.

The situation is like that illustrated in Figure 11. If we choose
a particular size (in terms of annual capacity) for the additions x,
each addition will satisfy the growth of demand for x/w years.

For reasons of mathematical simplicity, we choose to use a continuous discount factor e^{-rt}, where e is the natural logarithm base, r
is the continuous discount rate, and t is the time expressed in units
commensurate with the units of the discount rate. The continuous discount factor r is related to the usual, discrete time discount factor $(1/1 + i)^t$ in the way that semiannual, quarterly, or daily compounding of interest in a bank account is related to the annual
compounding of interest. If you deposit K_0 dollars at interest rate
i compounded annually, at the end of 1 year you will have

$$K_1 = K_0 (1 + i)$$

If the interest is compounded semiannually, the bank will compute the
balance of your account at the end of one year by the formula:

$$K_2 = K_0 (1 + i/2)^2$$

Compounded quarterly, the balance at the end of the year would be

$$K_4 = K_0 (1 + i/4)^4$$

and compounded daily it would be

$$K_{365} = K_0 (1 + i/365)^{365}$$

If we carry the process to the limit, letting the number of compoundings grow without bound, we would approach the following year-end value of the account,

$$K = \lim_{n \to \infty} K_n = \lim_{n \to \infty} K_0 (1 + i/n)^n$$

$$= K_0 e^i$$

Therefore, after t years, the value would be $K_0 e^{it}$. Similarly, if we wanted to discount the value K to the beginning value K_0, we could just compute

$$K_0 = K e^{-it}$$

which would be an example of continuous discounting from time t back to the present.

If we want to find the continuous discount rate r that will give us exactly the same discounted value as the discrete time discount rate i, we have the following relationship:

$$\frac{1}{(1 + i)^t} = e^{-rt}$$

Taking natural logarithms on both sides, we have

$$-t \log_e (1 + i) = -rt \quad \text{or} \quad \log_e (1 + i) = r$$

If we use a continuous discount factor e^{-rt}, the present value of all the costs associated with an indefinite sequence of additions of size x is given by

$$PVC = TC(x) + TC(x) e^{-rx/w} + TC(x) e^{-2rx/w} + \cdots \tag{A1}$$

$$PVC = TC(x) (1 + e^{-rx/w} + e^{-2rx/w} + \cdots) \tag{A2}$$

$$PVC = TC(x) [1/(1 - e^{-rx/w})] \tag{A3}$$

If the cost function has the appropriate mathematical properties, we can minimize PVC through an appropriate choice of size of addition x^*. The value x^* can be deduced by differentiating the function in equation A3 above and setting the derivative equal to zero. If we let

$g(x)$ stand for the ratio in (A3) and if we let primes designate first derivatives, the following rule for choosing the optimum size x^* can be derived: choose x^* so that

$$\frac{TC'(x^*)}{TC(x^*)} = \frac{-g'(x^*)}{g(x^*)} \tag{A4}$$

This problem is overly simplified, but it illustrates the mathematical modeling of a staging problem and the application of simple optimizing techniques to its solution.

7 SELECTED EMPIRICAL STUDIES

This chapter presents the results of particular applied studies that serve to illustrate and extend some of the points and problems discussed earlier in the book. In each case, parts of the relevant background and much of the analytical methodology have had to be omitted in the interests of brevity. The references to each case are given, however, so that the interested reader can pursue matters of particular interest to him. The purpose then is really to explore new avenues of analysis and new forms of data presentation to improve the comprehensiveness of the decision making process.

The first section presents three attempts actually to implement multiple objective planning. These procedures remain in a very formative state, but the approaches taken by these three teams, the way their data presentations were arranged, and the brief statements of some of the difficulties encountered should help other planners.

The section on the measurement of environmental impacts presents one illustration of the construction of an environmental index and inventory. It is important that the water manager know the quality and degree of uniqueness of the areas that his projects will affect. Since methods of environmental impact measurement are still so un-settled however, one particularly imaginative and suggestive case of the development of a specific environmental index dealing with river landscapes is presented.

The third section discusses further the problems of measuring benefits from water quality improvements. Agricultural, industrial, and municipal benefits are discussed and illustrated through empirical studies. The fourth section deals specifically with recreation benefits as a function of water quality. The final section is concerned with alternative ways of achieving stated water quality standards, the use of effluent charges, and some of the issues involved in establishing an effluent charge system.

Application of Multiple Objective Planning

In the summer of 1968, a special task force of the U.S. Water Resources Council began its work on the development of new and broadened procedures for evaluating water and related land resource projects. The appearance of the results of that work in July 1970 represented another addition to the now famous sequence of federal water policy and planning documents: the Flood Control Act of 1936, which enunciated the rule that project benefits should 'exceed the costs, to whomsoever they accrue'; the 1950 'Green Book' of the Federal Interagency River Basin Committee; Bureau of the Budget Circular A-47 of 1952; and *Policies, Standards, and Procedures in the Formulation, Evaluation, and Review of Plans for Use and Development of Water and Related Land Resources*, otherwise known as Senate Document 97 of 1962.

The U.S. Water Resources Council was established in 1965 as a permanent coordinating and guiding agency for federal water policy. Subject to the approval of the president, it is empowered to set the procedures to be followed by federal agencies in planning and evaluating water developments. The first major policy move of the council was to increase the discount rate to be used in evaluation procedures by tying it to current government bond yields.

The discount rate increase made many prospective federal water projects economically infeasible (i.e., it drove their B/C ratios below zero). This infeasibility served to reinforce a growing anxiety that existing evaluation procedures tended to slight the noneconomic effects of water projects, especially the environmental and regionally developmental impacts. These pressures for a more comprehensive view of water development benefits led the council to appoint a special task force to work on a multiple objective approach to evaluation and planning.

The deliberations of the special task force led to the publication of three documents (U.S. Water Resources Council, 1970a, b, c): *Principles for Planning Water and Land Resources* is a statement of a scheme for multiple objective planning; *Standards for Planning Water and Land Resources* provides definitions and measurement standards for benefits and costs, procedures for plan formulation, definition of national priorities, and so on; and *Findings and Recommendations* suggests official approval of the principles and standards as the basis for evaluation and planning by all federal agencies.

Multiple objective evaluation as formulated in *Principles for Planning Water and Land Resources* involves filling in the costs and benefits for four basic 'accounts': (1) national economic development (i.e., national economic efficiency); (2) quality of the environment; (3) social well-being (i.e., considerations of equitable distribution of income, population, employment, health, and so on, especially with respect to disadvantaged groups); and (4) regional development (i.e., positive and negative impacts occurring within a region some of which may net out of national effects, such as the migration of industry from one region to another). All these types of impacts can be fitted into the slightly more simplified four-objective framework presented in chapter 3.

The utility of these concepts was tested in a sequence of 19 field tests on actual or potential river basin development plans or projects during 1969-1970 (U.S. Water Resources Council, 1970d). Two of these tests are summarized below; for another test, see Schmid and Ward (1970). Considerably before the special task force had begun its deliberations, however, the U.S. Army Corps of Engineers, heading an interagency Susquehanna River basin study, had begun searching for a broader basis for planning and evaluation. The following text describes the outlines of that early effort and is taken from Werner (1968) with the author's kind consent.

The Susquehanna River Basin Study

'The basin is the largest on the Atlantic Seaboard of the United States with a drainage area of 27,500 square miles. The river has its origin in New York State and flows some 450 miles to the Chesapeake Bay. About eighty per cent of the basin drainage is in Pennsylvania and comprises forty-six per cent of the state. Most of the remainder of the basin is in New York with but a small portion in the state of Maryland. Maryland, however, counts on water from the Susquehanna as a major source of the water supply of its largest city, Baltimore. The river also has a major but not too well understood effect on Maryland's most important natural resource, the Chesapeake Bay....

'The basin included developed areas exhibiting vigorous economic growth and other areas where various combinations of conditions had resulted in a depressed economy. About eighty per cent of the basin was in Appalachia as defined in the Appalachian Regional Development Act. Waters of the region varied in quality from Lake Otsego where Cooperstown, New York drew its water supply untreated, to streams such as Lackawanna where acid mine drainage made the water unfit for use in municipal or industrial water supply without special treatment....Some reaches of the stream had the more common quality problems caused by inadequately treated municipal and industrial wastes. Some coal mining areas exhibited the visual blight of large smoking culm piles adjacent to towns and scars of strip mining operations. There were also natural values in the basin of considerable regional importance and two major stretches of the river had been recommended for consideration as des- ignation as national scenic rivers....

'*Evolution of multiple-objective planning for the Susquehanna study.* In September, 1966, the Secretary of the Army directed the Chief of Engineers to form a task force to review the Susquehanna River Basin Study to determine if the standards recommended by the Civil Works Study Board were being met with respect to the treatment of planning alternatives....The task force after much discussion concluded that the then current plan of study of the Susquehanna Study would not adequately treat planning alternatives as envisioned by the Civil Works Study Board. The Susquehanna plan of study as- sured "mainly the formulation of an economic efficiency plan modified by consideration of the objectives of the three states involved, in- cluding some consideration of equity and acceptability." The task force also concluded that study objectives, identified in the plan of study, of regional development, economic efficiency and preservation appeared "to be sufficiently varied and fundamentally different to offer an adequate basis for discussion and choice," provided plans of equal detail were developed in pursuit of each objective....

'The task force report was completed in November, 1966, and revised in April, 1967. The findings of the task force were first presented to the Susquehanna Study Coordinating Committee on April 17,
1967. By letter in July of 1967, the chairman of the coordinating
committee proposed ... formulation of a demonstration or base plan
for the basin -- this would be a least-cost, but conventionally formulated plan to meet the study-developed needs of the basin. Further,
it was proposed that the base plan would be modified to meet each of
the three objectives of economic efficiency, regional development and
what was then termed environmental control. A separate plan would be
developed in support of each of the three defined objectives. The
concluding step in plan formulation would be selection by the coordinating committee of a plan formulated from features of the three
single objective plans and presented in the final study report in its
relationship to the other three plans....

... One question raised was whether it was worth while spending
time developing three plans when only one, that of regional development, was likely to be acceptable in the basin. Another point made
was that a broad array of alternatives could be confusing to the public and disruptive when it came time to seek support of a recommended
course of action. Consensus was finally reached that the three-plan
approach would be applied to three sub-basins....

'*Objectives and criteria for the Susquehanna study*. The Susquehanna Study Group at Baltimore District with some outside assistance
defined the objectives for the multiple-objective approach to planning proposed for use in the Susquehanna River Basin study....

'The economic efficiency objective was defined for the coordinating committee: "Return the maximum in social and economic satisfaction through investment in water resource restoration and development from the viewpoint of the nation as a whole." Other documents
amplified the definition. The plan was to attempt to maximize net
national benefits. "The plan will constitute a benchmark against
which other plans ... can be evaluated." The plan might include some
features of plans in support of other objectives to the extent that

such features were considered to be a national objective or in the
national interest. In deciding what should be included or excluded,
value judgments would have to be made by the planners....

'Regional development as a planning objective was defined: "Return
the maximum in social and economic satisfaction through investment in
water resource restoration and development from the viewpoint of the
Susquehanna River Basin." ... Regional development as an objective
was intended to be defined by the regional study participants to be
responsive to what were believed to be regional needs and aspira-
tions....

'Environmental quality was defined: "return the maximum in social
and economic satisfaction through investment in water resources restoration and development, with emphasis on minimum disturbance of the
natural environment and on restoration and enhancement of environmental and aesthetic values." ...

'In the formulation of each of the objective-related plans for the
Susquehanna River sub-basin, the same study-developed basin "needs"
for water-related goods and services were taken as "given." Using
the criteria associated with the three selected objectives, each plan
was developed to meet, to some degree, this single set of basin needs.
One advantage was that a common basis for comparison was available
among the three plans. A common basis for comparison could become
quite important as plan formulation rapidly became complicated, particularly as the basin or sub-basin was operated as a system. A
simple sub-basin with many potential storage sites, each with a non-
linear storage-cost function being evaluated for perhaps five purposes, rapidly would become too difficult for man or machine to man-
age without simplifying assumptions. Another advantage of having
each plan treat a certain set of basin needs was that the plans also
met a concern expressed by the coordinating committee regarding im-
plementability. Each plan proposed, if implemented, could be said to
have met the (given) needs of the basin with regard to water use to
some greater or lesser degree.

'There were disadvantages to this procedure also. One was the assumption of validity of the particular standard or need. Basin needs

were developed from a series of studies, and calculations and each
successive study usually had its own explicit or implicit assumptions.
The disadvantage of having all plans on a common base was that the
basic structural derivation of needs was not questioned .... A second
disadvantage was that within each plan a number of compromises or
trade-offs would have already been made before the single objective
plan was brought before the coordinating committee. For instance, in
formulating the environmental quality plan, decisions would necessarily have been made regarding preservation versus development.

'The plans are summarized in Table [6]. A possible "plan" that
was discussed but which did not materialize was the zero plan -- the
situation where no water resource development was undertaken. The
development of such a plan or, more accurately, the appraisal of regional effects in the absence of any development plan, would have provided an interesting basis for discussing alternative schemes of development. In the absence of such an approach, the economic efficiency plan appeared as the neutral plan -- the plan that would provide (at least cost) the water and water controls assumed in the economic base study projections.'

*Cornell University Study of the Stonewall Jackson Reservoir, West Fork
River, West Virginia*

This study was one of the test cases contracted for by the U.S.
Water Resources Council to test the feasibility of *Principles for
Planning Water and Land Resources* and *Standards for Planning Water
and Land Resources*. Tables 7 through 11 (Kalter et al., 1970) illustrate the types of analytical results that it is now possible to generate for a project.

The Stonewall Jackson Reservoir site is located in northern West
Virginia in the headwaters area of the Monongahela River basin. The
dam itself has been authorized for flood control, water supply, water
quality control, and recreation. The annual economic efficiency benefits and costs originally estimated by the U.S. Army Corps of Engineers were $2,464,000 and $1,442,000, respectively. The project was
authorized in 1966 and is in the advanced planning stage.

TABLE 6. Susquehanna River Basin Study Summary for Plans for Subbasins 1, 2, and 3

Project Type	Economic Efficiency Plan		Regional Development Plan		Environmental Quality Plan	
	Number of Projects	Cost, 10^3/yr	Number of Projects	Cost, 10^3/yr	Number of Projects	Cost, 10^3/yr
Reservoirs (major)*	9	7,805	14	16,820	5	8,040
Reservoirs (minor)*	49	3,900	94	5,180	57	2,635
Groundwater well fields	5	1,465	3	565	7	2,340
Diversion pipelines	1	2,420	1	2,420	1	2,420
Diversion sewer lines	...	...	...	...	...	...
Advanced waste treatment	4	540	3	290	6	770
Mine drainage watersheds	2	610	3	5,310	3	7,260
Land treatment, 10^3 acres						
Agricultural	995	2,370	995	2,370	995	2,370
Forest	735	775	735	775	735	775
Pastureland	630	2,210	630	2,210	630	2,210
Reclamation	21	1,055	21	1,055	21	1,055
Bank stabilization	...	...	...	...	...	...
Local flood protection	...	...	4	125	1	100
Floodplain management	moderate		low to moderate		moderate to intense	
Low (channel) dam use	...		moderate in one subbasin		moderate to substantial	
Small urban recreation	...	...	...	...	30	+
Total Cost		22,750		37,120		29,975

Table adapted from Werner (1968). All figures are tentative.
* Major and minor refer to the size of watershed served.

TABLE 7.   Benefit-Cost Data for
Stonewall Jackson Reservoir

Initial Investment

First cost	$33,486,000
Interest during construction	2,450,000
@ 4 7/8%	
Total	35,936,000

Average Annual Charges

Interest (4 7/8%)	1,752,000
Amortization (100-year life)	31,800
Operation and maintenance	146,700
Major replacements	17,000
Total	1,947,500

Average Annual Benefits

Recreation	479,000
Water supply	191,900
Flood control	765,000
Employment benefits	137,000
Subtotal	1,572,900
Adjustment for net loss	-111,000
of productivity on land	
Total	$1,461,900

Table adapted from Kalter et al. (1970, Table 1).

Reestimates of the national economic efficiency benefits and costs
by the Cornell team are shown in Table 7.   A discount rate of 4 7/8%
was used.   The results implied are a B/C ratio of 0.75 and a present
value of net efficiency benefits (B - C) of -$9,533,000.   The project
clearly was unjustified economically.

The investigators followed their initial economic efficiency analysis with a sensitivity analysis of the B/C ratio and present worth
of the project as they relate to variations in annual benefits and
initial investments.   Three alternative values for annual benefits
and for initial investment (original estimates, 10% increase, 10% decrease) were combined to make nine possible outcomes, the implications
of which were calculated in terms of B/C and (B - C).   This procedure
was considered a way of quantifying the possible uncertainties in the
estimates.   The results are shown in Table 8.   The sensitivity test
results certainly did not indicate any possibility that the potential

TABLE 8. Criterion Sensitivity to Changes in
Initial Investment and Annual Benefits

Annual Benefits	Initial Investment	Economic Measures	
		B/C	B-C,$
Original	Original	0.75	-9,533
Original	10% Increase	0.69	-13,127
Original	10% Decrease	0.83	-5,940
10% Increase	Original	0.83	-6,960
10% Decrease	Original	0.68	-12,506
10% Increase	10% Increase	0.76	-10,154
10% Increase	10% Decrease	0.92	-2,966
10% Decrease	10% Increase	0.62	-16,100
10% Decrease	10% Decrease	0.75	-8,913

Table adapted from Kalter et al. (1970, Table 2). Economic measures based on 100-year time horizon and 4 7/8% discount rate.

ranges of uncertainty in benefit and cost estimates could change the conclusion that the project was economically unjustified.

The investigators followed the sensitivity analysis with an analysis of benefits and costs as they would accrue to the region. The first task was to define the relevant region, for benefits tend to cluster around the project, whereas costs tend to be more widely spread. As a matter of judgment, it was decided to define the region as that area surrounding the project site and including all land and communities directly affected by the flood control and water supply features.

Isolating regional benefits and costs was conceived of as requiring three basic steps: (1) to determine what part of the net national economic efficiency benefits accrued to the region; (2) to determine the extent to which the growth rate and future incomes of the region would be changed; (3) to determine 'multiplier' effects of the project in the region, i.e., the effects that take the form of industry moving into the region from elsewhere as a result of the project. Steps 2 and 3 are not clearly distinct, since regional growth may well take the form of attracting activities from elsewhere. There is also the question of whether regions other than the project region should be analyzed for (possibly adverse) project related impacts. (See Howe

TABLE 9. Present Value Regional Impacts from Primary
Functions, Stonewall Jackson Reservoir

Function	Present Value Gross Benefits,$	Present Value Costs,$	Present Value Net Benefits,$
Flood control	15,558,598	13,429	15,545,169
Water supply	3,863,836	1,625,718	2,238,118
Recreation	4,870,959	2,454,058	2,416,901
Total	24,293,393	4,093,205	20,200,188

Table adapted from Kalter et al. (1970, Table 16). Present value
costs include investment costs and operation, maintenance, and repair costs.

and Easter (1971) for extended discussions of the impacts of the expansion of irrigated agriculture on other regions.) The analysis of
regional net benefits from the project is summarized in Table 9.

Following the isolation of net benefits to the region, an analysis
of the distribution of these regional benefits among the different
household income classes was carried out. To accomplish this, it was
necessary to (1) assign costs directly borne by project users to the
various income classes, (2) assign costs indirectly borne through
federal taxation, and (3) assign the regional benefits from flood
control, water supply, and recreation. Naturally these procedures
involved substantial data gathering; were based in part on some necessary assumptions about the incidence of benefits; and required extended analysis, the details of which can be found in the report itself. The summary presentation of the income distribution data is
shown in Table 10.

Finally, the Cornell team stated the following concerning environmental impacts (Kalter et al., 1970, pp. 62-63):

'... With respect to natural resources, terms like prevention,
preservation and protection have been associated with the "Conservation Movement" throughout its history. These terms are emphasized
when the Task Force Report cites the types of environmental quality
effects to be considered in planning water development projects. The
four types of effects cited are: (1) The preservation or enhancement

TABLE 10.   Net Benefit Distribution of the Stonewall Jackson
Project by Regional Income Class

Income Class,$	Present Value of Net Benefit,$	Net Benefits by Income Class,%	Net Benefits per Household,$
<3,000	4,473,017	22	458
3,000 to 10,000	12,922,456	64	550
>10,000	2,804,715	14	659
Total	20,200,188	100	...

Table adapted from Kalter et al. (1970, Table 14).

of aesthetic areas; (2) the protection of areas of archaelogical, historical, or scientific value; (3) the protection or enhancement of water quality; and (4) the prevention of erosion and the restoration of eroded areas with particular emphasis on the treatments of watersheds, mined areas, and critical erosion areas. In effect, the environmental quality account is to facilitate the specific expression of the "Conservation" consequences of a water development project ....

'Because of problems associated with the measurement of quality differences with respect to the environment, the analyst of governmental investment has been restricted, at best, to placing monetary values on this type of impact. An environmental quality change is often classified as a technological externality and measured in either physical or value terms. Once so classified and quantified, the impact can logically be included as part of a benefit-cost analysis for the national economic efficiency account. Since a water development project may produce, as well as correct, adverse or beneficial effects on the environment, which in turn influence the consumption or production pattern of others due to physical linkages, the value of the externalities is a relevant consideration. However, not all such impacts can be measured nor does such a definition delimit the meaning of environmental quality. Thus, an economic efficiency analysis cannot fully express the environmental quality effects. Because of this, a separate environmental account is justified in which the effects are specified in physical, rather than value, terms.'

The final display of environmental quality impacts given by the
Cornell team is shown as Table 11.

University of Michigan Analysis of Alternative Development Plans for The Susquehanna River

The basic problem with multiple objective planning is that we do
not know the appropriate weights to assign to the different objectives, even if we think we can measure the degree of attainment of
those objectives. As a result (and as suggested earlier in chapter
3), it may be desirable to design several alternative plans, each em-
phasizing a different objective. This design of alternative plans
was the idea of the interagency Susquehanna study presented at the
beginning of this chapter.

If alternative designs are produced, how can they best be compared?
The work of a team from the University of Michigan on a hypothetical
river development illustrates one very workable approach. The methodology of the team is best expressed in its own words (Schramm and
Burt, 1970, p. 26):

'Given multiple, frequently competitive goals -- such as those implied in the four accounts -- which plan, or which range of alternative plans, should be developed for presentation to the Administration
and Congress? The proposed Task Force procedures are not clear on
that point. On the one hand, they recommend as an acceptable approach
"the method of optimizing one objective within specifically prescribed
constraints for other objectives," but on the other they express the
hope that "eventually a more advanced system of optimization based on
weighting of the different objectives may be possible of development."
The first approach would imply that four separate plans, one for each
of the four accounts suggested by the Task Force, would have to be
drawn up. Each of these four alternatives would maximize its particular objective subject to minimum acceptable levels acting as constraints with respect to the other three objectives. Such a procedure
begs the question of what the constraint level for the other objectives should be and what the marginal benefits or costs of relaxing or
tightening these constraints would be in terms of all other objectives. This issue is discussed in greater detail in the following

TABLE 11. Environmental Quality Display,
Stonewall Jackson Reservoir

Beneficial Consequences	Detrimental Consequences

Recreation and Commercial Area

1. Primitive camping on the small islands produced by the dam.	1. Inundation of the picturesque wooded and grassland hillsides which are not unique in the region.
2. Possible establishment of a medium quality reservoir fishery.	2. Inundation of a low quality stream fishery - 35.1 miles.
3. The improvement in the scenery for recreation related commercial enterprises.	

Scientific and Historic Area

1. The reservoir and the wildlife mitigation area could serve as a natural ecological laboratory. How-However, these areas are not scientifically unique.	1. Inundation of old farms with possible historic value.

Water Quality Area

1. Reduction in hardness concentration of 5.3 mg/l for an average of 151 days annually on the Monongahela River and 69 mg/l for an average of 241 days on the West Fork River when the reservoir release is greater than 100 cfs (cubic feet per second).	1. Inundation of natural gas pipes which leaves the reservoir liable to underwater leaks.
2. Decrease in acid concentration by 2.7 mg/l for a period of 168 days in the Monongahela River and 7 mg/l over a period of 277 days in the West Fork River when the reservoir flow is 150 cfs.	2. There is no increase in organic assimilation capacity because of the reservoir.
3. The acid reduction will prevent corrosion to locks, barges, boats, and dams by the amount equivalent to $6,000 annually when the flow is 100 cfs.	3. There is double counting of some flood control and water supply benefits on the West Fork River because of the duplicating effects of the reservoir and two small watershed projects.
4. Water temperature on the Monongahela River will be controlled by flow regulation such that annual benefit is equal to $11,000.	

Table adapted from Kalter et al. (1970, Table 18).

section. The second procedure suggests that only a single, "optimum"
plan would be drawn up and presented. This plan would be developed
by assigning appropriate weights to the various objectives. The Task
Force procedures suggest that these weights could be established a
priori by stating:

> The recommendations for relative emphasis to be given various ob-
> jectives would be submitted to the Council, the President, and the
> Congress for use when drafting directives for detailed planning
> studies.

'As will be pointed out in the following section, it is rather unlikely that such a general weighting scheme of social objectives could
be drawn up in advance and retain its validity in the face of the
unique combination of multiple objectives facing a planner at different points in time ....

'There is, however, a more appropriate method available to account
for the real costs, albeit not for the benefits, of non-monetary, non-
national income objectives. This method would utilize the actual reductions in potential total net national income benefits as a yardstick of the costs of achieving non-national income objectives.

'What is required for this purpose is, as a first step, the development of an objective function which has as its single goal the
maximization of net national income benefits. This function should
not be subject to any explicit or implicit constraints with respect to
other, non-national income goals. As a result, the function will indicate what the largest net national income gain could be from the development of a given water resource. This national efficiency function will provide the planner with a yardstick that can be used to
measure the opportunity costs of other non-monetary or non-quantifi-
able purposes. If on the other hand, the latter were incorporated
directly into a single planning function there would be no way to
measure the resulting true losses in efficiency. But these losses --
if any -- are the only real national income costs that can be legit-
imately assigned to the achievement of all other objectives. For cost
allocation purposes alone, therefore, it is necessary to know the unconstrained national income gains available from any given water

resource development. Once this national efficiency function has
been established, other alternatives can be developed which are designed with other objectives in mind such as improved income distribution or enhancement of environmental quality. The national income
costs of these objectives can then be measured by the difference in
net national income benefits between the single-objective efficiency
function and its various, multi-objective alternatives.

'Three issues must be kept in mind in the interpretation and use of
the national efficiency function. First, given the multiple objectives of water resources planning there is no reason whatsoever to
consider the development pattern resulting in the largest gain of net
national income as a particularly desirable alternative that should,
somehow, have preference over other alternatives which incorporate
broader objectives.

'Second, there is no reason to insist on limiting the choice of appropriate alternatives to those which show a national income benefit-
cost ratio of equal to or greater than one. It may well be that there
are alternatives available which result in a net national income loss.
In terms of broader social objectives, however, the losses in national
income could be more than compensated for by other, non-income gains.
Examples of such alternatives would be preservation and managed improvement of wilderness areas, creation of new national parks with
limited visitor accessability, improvements in water quality that are
not matched by equal increases in measurable economic benefits, or
particularly favorable effects on income distributional patterns.

'Third, the reductions in net national income gains as measured by
the efficiency function only measure the national income costs of
achieving other goals and objectives. They do not provide a positive
assessment of the real value of any of those goals. The question
whether the latter are worth less, the same or more than the amount
of national income gains foregone will have to remain a matter of
judgment by policy makers in each and every case.'

Having proposed the basic strategy of developing an optimum national economic efficiency plan (called by the team the 'national

income maximization plan') and using it as the benchmark from which
the economic costs of achieving other objectives can be measured, the
team proceeded to display the results of two alternative plans in the
manner indicated in Tables 12, 13, 14, 15, and 16.

Given that the distribution of project benefits and costs, environmental impacts, and other types of impact on human well-being are to
be taken into account in developing plans alternative to the national
economic efficiency plan, the question still remains as to the procedures for arriving at alternative plans. The Michigan team concluded
that, in most cases, it would suffice to start with the optimum economic efficiency design and to look then for the most advantageous
trade offs of economic net benefits for the achievement of other goals
(e.g., lowering the dam height a bit to preserve a scenic meadow, increasing water quality more to permit sports, fishing, and so on).
However, for special cases in which, for example, unique environments
are involved, decisions

> ...require a national and national-regional inventory of environ-
> mental (aesthetic-visual, ecological and historical human-interest
> resources and resource demands. It should be noted that the weight
> attached to any one of them will vary not only on the basis of na-
> tional standards but also by region, depending on the environmental
> factor's regional uniqueness characteristics. A mature forest in
> western Texas might have high environmental values to the region
> where its equivalent in Oregon might have value only as a stand
> of commercial timber (Schramm and Burt, 1970, p. 32).

Measurement of Environmental Impacts

> On property we grow pigs or peanuts. On land we grow suburbs
> or sunflowers. On landscape we grow feelings or frustrations.
> (Leopold and Marchand, 1968).

Many aspects of our intrusions into the environment are difficult
to describe. How do we compare the impacts of two alternative pipe-
line routes across the face of a hill? How do we judge whether a reservoir or the preservation of a natural river constitutes the greatest
contribution to environmental enhancement?

Often such questions are answered only by the anguished outcries of
highly interested groups with quite different and unreconcilable value

TABLE 12. Plan 1: Unconstrained National Income
Maximization Plan for an Example River Site
Showing Benefits

Output Category	Evaluation Basis	Price Basis	Present Value, 10^6

Electric power
  Example dam site
  Downstream benefits
    to existing plants
    A, B, and C
	Production and delivery costs of alternative thermal plant	Estimated 1974 price basis plus 3% p.a. estimated increase in costs of alternative thermal plant	20.0
			5.0

Irrigation	Estimated increase in net farm income (increased value of gross output minus all increases in farm operating costs; cost exclude capital costs)	Estimated 1974 price basis plus 1½% p.a. estimated annual price increase	25.0
Recreation Nonpriced benefits	Imputed net benefits	Estimated 1974 value $1.50 per visitor day plus 2% p.a. rise in consumer price index	25.0
Unemployment and underemployment benefits	Difference in income of beneficiaries between the with and without case	1971 wage level plus estimated 6% p.a. rise in money wages	5.0
Total gross benefits			80.0

Table adapted from Schramm and Burt (1970, Table 1). Table
presents a 50-year analysis with hypothetical data. Discount
rate used for all categories is 4 7/8%.

TABLE 13. Plan 1: Unconstrained National Income
Maximization Plan on an Example River Site
Showing Costs

Item	Costs Paid by	Price Basis	Discount Rate,%	Present Value, 10^6		
				Investment	OM and R	Total
Dam and reservoir	federal	1970 plus 3% inflator	4 7/8	9.0	1.0	10.0
General property acquisition	federal state	1970 1970	4 7/8 6 1/2	8.0 2.0	... ...	8.0 2.0
Power plant	federal	1970 plus 3% p.a. inflator	4 7/8	6.0	4.0	10.0
Transmission	private	1970 plus 4% p.a. inflator	8 1/2	1.5	0.5	2.0
Pumping plant and canals	federal	1970 plus 3% p.a. inflator	4 7/8	3.0	1.0	4.0
Irrigation facilities and equipment	private	1970 plus 3% p.a. inflator	11	4.0	...	4.0
Recreation facilities	federal state	1970 plus 3% p.a. inflator	4 7/8 6 1/2	0.5 0.5	2.0 2.0	2.5 2.5
Roads, sewage, water supply	state local	1970 plus 2½% p.a. inflator	6 1/2 7 1/2	2.0 1.0	1.0 1.0	3.0 2.0
Total costs				37.5	12.5	50.0

Table adapted from Schramm and Burt (1970, Table 2). Table presents
a 50-year analysis with hypothetical data.

systems. Certainly more objective information would help in reconciling opposed viewpoints and in strengthening the hand of the public decision maker.

A very interesting example of how such information can be generated
is found in Leopold (1969). Leopold develops what he calls a 'uniqueness index' that could be highly useful to the planner in comparing
potential development sites.

TABLE 14.   Plan 2: Alternative Development Plan A on an
Example River Site Showing National Income Benefits

Output Category	Factors Considered in Comparison to Plan 1	Net Output Changes Compared to Plan 1	Total Value of Output
		Present Value,10^6	
Electric power			
Example dam site	Environment	-3.0*	
	Social well-being	-1.0†	16.0
Downstream benefits	Environment	-1.5*	
to existing plants A, B, and C	Social well-being	-0.5†	3.0
Irrigation	Environment	-3.0*	
	Social well-being	-1.5†	
	Income-distribution	-0.5§	20.0
Recreation	Environment	+3.0*	28.0
Unemployment and underemployment benefits	Environment	-1.0*	4.0
Total national income benefits			71.0

Table taken from Schramm and Burt (1970, Table 4).   Table presents
a 50-year analysis with hypothetical data.
   * Output reductions for environmental enhancement equal $-5.5
million.
   † Output reductions for social well-being improvements equal $-3.0
million.
   § Output reductions for income distribution improvements equal $-0.5
million.

   Leopold surveyed 12 streams in central Idaho, including the stretch
of the Snake River flowing through Hells Canyon. For each stream, he
recorded 46 characteristics or 'factors,' each assigned a value from
1 to 5 according to a scheme illustrated in Table 17.

   Each stream thus is assigned a value of 1 to 5 for each of 46 factors. The values for this case are shown in Table 18. Leopold considered a stream 'more unique' with respect to a particular factor the
fewer the number of streams sharing the same value assigned to that
factor. For example, with respect to depth at low flow (Table 18),
stream 2 was the only one assigned value of 3, whereas six out of the
12 streams had values of 2, two had values of 4, and three had values

TABLE 15. Plan 2: Alternative Development Plan A on an
Example River Site Showing National Income Costs

| Item | Cost Paid by | Present Value,$10^6 | | | |
		Basic Investment Costs	Investment Cost Changes	OM and R	Total Costs
Dam and reservoir	federal	8.0	+2.0*	1.0	11.0
General property acquisition	federal	7.0	+1.0*	...	
	state	2.0	+1.0†	...	
			+0.5§	...	9.5
			+0.5§	...	2.5
Power plant	federal	5.5	+1.0*	4.0	10.5
Transmission	private	1.5	+1.0*	0.5	3.0
Pumping plant and canals	federal	2.8	+1.0†		
			+0.7*	1.0	5.5
Irrigation facilities and equipment	private	4.0	+0.5†	...	4.5
Recreation facilities	federal	0.8	+0.7*	2.0	3.5
	state	0.8	+0.7§	2.0	3.5
Roads, sewers, water supply	state	2.0		1.0	3.0
	local	1.0		1.0	2.0
Total basic costs		35.4		12.5	
Total national income costs					58.5

Table adapted from Schramm and Burt (1970, Table 5). Table presents a 50-year analysis with hypothetical data.

* These investment cost changes are in consideration of environment. Total costs for environmental enhancement equal $6.4 million.

† These investment cost changes are in consideration of income distribution improvements. Total costs for income distribution improvements equal $2.5 million.

§ These investment cost changes are in consideration of social well-being improvements. Total costs for social well-being improvements equal $1.7 million.

of 5. Stream 2 would thus be assigned a 'uniqueness ratio' with respect to depth at low flow of 1/1 = 1.0, whereas six of the streams would have a uniqueness ratio with respect to that factor of 1/6 = 0.17. All the uniqueness ratios are summarized in Table 19. Naturally, there exists an infinite number of ways of combining the 46

TABLE 16.   Net National Income Costs of Social Objectives
Incorporated in Alternative Plan A

| Social Objective | Total National Income Costs, Present Value,$10^6 | | |
	Cost-Adjusted Reductions in Benefits	Additional Separable Costs	Total Costs
Environment	4.3	6.4	10.7
Social well-being	2.1	1.7	3.8
Income distribution	0.5	2.5	3.0
Total national income reductions for all other social purposes			17.5

Table adapted from Schramm and Burt (1970, Table 7, part 3).

uniqueness ratios of each stream into one index of the overall uniqueness of that stream.   Leopold chose merely to add the ratios over subsets of the factors and over all factors (Tables 20 and 21).   The
total index provides a ranking of streams by uniqueness.   Uniqueness
is just that: it is neither a measure of good nor of bad.   For example,
stream site 7 has the greatest uniqueness by the index but is, in fact,
the only sluggish, algae-infested, murky stream of the group.   Stream
site 5 with an index of 16.09 ranks second and is the Snake River in
Hells Canyon.   Obviously, the index must be interpreted in the context
of the sample stream sites being ranked.

A question naturally arises concerning the universe of streams to
which a given stream should be compared.   The universe of streams
could be all those streams in North America or only those in central
Idaho.   This framework for comparison is in part a matter of judgment
and in part a function of whether the decision at hand relates to regional or national welfare.   Such indices of the various dimensions
of the environment would be extremely valuable to the rational decision-making process.

Benefits from Water Quality Improvement

One of the most difficult tasks in the water quality field is to
assess the benefits that would be forthcoming from different degrees
of water quality improvement.   Activities that could benefit from

quality improvement are agriculture, industry, municipalities, and
water recreation.

Problems of water quality (i.e., degradation adversely affecting
agriculture) are found primarily in the arid parts of the southwestern
United States where increasing salinity of irrigation water, particularly in the Colorado River, is projected to reduce yields of irrigated crops. Pincock (1969) has estimated some of the damages that
are likely to result from projected salinity levels at the point where
Colorado River water is diverted for the Wellton-Mohawk irrigation
district in Yuma County, Arizona. The total dissolved solids (TDS)
level for 1960 was 800 ppm, and the projections indicated a level of
920 ppm for 1980 and 1233 ppm for 2010. Yield reductions projected
for 1980 were negligible, but the following gross dollar losses per
acre (in 1960 dollars) were estimated for the year 2010 (Pincock,
1969, Table 5):

Alfalfa	2.10	Lettuce	74.26
Alfalfa seed	1.00	Lemons	18.45
Melons	12.72	Grapefruit	13.32
	Oranges	27.68	

The gross annual loss in value of output for the entire district was
estimated to be $854,657 by 2010, the net loss being $464,000 after
reduced expenses were taken into account.

Clearly, these losses are not going to be trivial in the future.
Other areas, such as the Imperial and Coachella Valleys in California,
will also be affected in some degree, as will the activities (e.g.,
recreation, fishing) dependent on the Salton Sea, the ultimate depos-
itory of the return flows from the Imperial Valley's irrigation water.
The adverse effects on the Mexicali region of Mexico are strongly evi-
dent and will cause increasing friction between the United States and
Mexico in the future.

The impact of intake water quality on industry has not been studied
extensively. The dominant fact seems to be that most of industry's
withdrawals are for cooling purposes, a function for which quality is
unimportant. Naturally, extreme conditions of acidity or alkalinity
could cause serious damage to cooling surfaces. In fact, a very low

TABLE 17. Field Evaluation of Aesthetic Factors at Selected Sites, Hells Canyon Area, Idaho; Evaluation Numbers for Descriptive Categories

Factor No.	Descriptive categories	Evaluation numbers of descriptive categories				
		1	2	3	4	5
	Physical factors:					
1	River width at low flow...ft..	<3	3 to 10	10 to 30	30 to 100	>100.
2	Depth at low flow...ft..	<.5	.5 to 1	1 to 2	2 to 5	>5.
3	Velocity at low flow...ft..	<.5	.5 to 1	1 to 2	3 to 5	>5.
4	Bankfull depth...ft..	<.1	.1 to 2	2 to 4	4 to 8	>8.
5	Flow variability	Little variation	Little variation	Normal	Ephemeral or large variation.	Ephemeral or large variation.
6	River pattern	Torrent	Pool and riffle	Without riffles	Meander	Braided.
7	Ratio of valley height to width.	≧1	2 to 5	5 to 10	11 to 14	≦15.
8	Bed material...mm	Clay or silt	Sand	Mixture of sand and gravel.	Gravel	Cobbles or larger.
9	Bed slope...ft per ft..	<.0005	.0005 to .001	.001 to .005	.005 to .01	>.01.
10	Basin area...sq mi..	<1	1 to 10	10 to 100	100 to 1,000	>1,000.
11	Stream order.	≧2	3	4	5	≦6.
12	Erosion of banks	Stable		Slumping		Eroding.
13	Deposition	Stable				Large-scale deposition.
14	Width of valley flat...ft..	<100	100 to 300	300 to 500	500 to 1,000	>1,000.
15	Water color:	Clear and colorless.		Green tints		Brown.
	Biologic and water quality:					
16	Turbidity...mg/1..	<25	25 to 150	150 to 1,000	1,000 to 5,000	>5,000.
17	Floating material	None	Vegetation	Foamy	Oily	Variety.
18	Water condition	Poor		Good		Excellent.
	Algae:					
19	Amount	Absent				Infested.
20	Type	Green on rocks	Blue green	Diatom	Floating green	None.
	Larger plants:					
21	Amount	Absent				Infested.
22	Kind	None	Unknown rooted	Elodea and duckweed.	Water lily	Cattail.
23	River fauna	None				Large variety.
24	Pollution evidence	None				Evident.
	Land flora:					
25	Valley	Open	Open with grass and trees.	Bushy	Wooded	Trees and brush.
26	Hillslope	Open	Open with grass and trees.	Brushy	Wooded	Trees and brush.
27	Diversity	Small				Great.
28	Condition	Good				Overused.
	Human use and interest: Number of occurences of trash and litter per 100 ft of river:					
29	Metal	<2	2 to 5	5 to 10	10 to 50	>50.

TABLE 17. (continued)

Factor No.	Descriptive categories	Evaluation numbers of descriptive categories				
		1	2	3	4	5
30	Paper	<2	2 to 5	5 to 10	10 to 50	>50.
31	Other	<2	2 to 5	5 to 10	10 to 50	>50.
32	Material removable	Easily removed				Difficult.
33	Artificial controls	Free and natural				Controlled.
	Accessibility:					
34	Individual	Wilderness				Urban or paved access.
35	Mass use	Wilderness				Urban or paved access.
36	Local scene	Diverse views and scenes				Closed or without diversity.
37	Vistas	Vistas of far places				Closed or no vistas.
38	View confinement	Open or no obstructions.				Closed by hills, cliffs, or trees.
39	Land use	Wilderness	Grazed	Lumbering	Forest and mixed recreation.	Urbanized.
40	Utilities	Scene unobstructed by power or electric lines.				Scene obstructed by utilities.
41	Degree of change	Original.				Materially altered.
42	Recovery potential	Natural recovery				Natural change unlikely.
43	Urbanization	No buildings				Many houses and buildings.
44	Special views	None				Unusual interest.
45	Historic features	None				Many.
46	Misfits	None				Many.

Table taken from Leopold (1969, Table 1).

TABLE 18. Category Assignment for Aesthetic Factors at the 12 Localities on Idaho Rivers

Category assigned to factors at indicated sites

Descriptive categories	1	2	3	4	5	6	7	8	9	10	11	12
Physical factors:												
River width at low flow												
Depth at low flow												
Velocity at low flow												
Bankfull depth												
Flow variability												
River pattern												
Ratio of valley height to width												
Bed material												
Bed slope												
Basin area												
Stream order												
Erosion of banks												
Deposition												
Width of valley flat												
Biologic and water quality:												
Water color												
Turbidity												
Floating material												
Water condition												
Algae:												
Amount												
Type												
Larger plants:												
Amount												
Kind												
River fauna												
Pollution evidence												
Land flora:												
Valley												
Hillslope												
Diversity												
Condition												
Human use and interest:												
Trash and litter:												
Metal												
Paper												
Other												
Material removable												
Artificial controls												
Accessibility:												
Individual												
Mass use												
Local scene:												
Vistas												
View confinement												
Land use												
Utilities												
Degree of change												
Recovery potential												
Urbanization												
Special views												
Historic features												
Misfits												

Table taken from Leopold (1969, Table 2). Category number (1-5) for each site indicates the range in which the measured or estimated quantity falls.

level of dissolved oxygen can reduce corrosion in evaporators. The
Sparrows Point plant of Bethlehem Steel buys a large part of Baltimore's sewage effluent for cooling purposes.

Frankel (1965) has studied the impact of upstream domestic sewage
discharges on the costs of required municipal treatment downstream
(Table 22). Frankel concluded that, if quality impacts on instream
uses between the discharge and intake points are not important, higher
degrees of treatment for domestic sewage discharges would not be economically justified by the savings in downstream intake treatment
costs unless the volume of upstream discharge became very large relative to the intake volume: in the ratio range of 16:1 to 250:1 for
small sewage treatment plants and 10:1 to 30:1 for large sewage treatment plants. The primary economic justification for higher degrees of
treatment of domestic sewage will in most cases be found in the beneficial impacts of improved quality on other stream uses: recreation,
fish life, and general esthetic considerations. This analysis does
not deal with industrial waste discharges.

Recreation Benefits from Water Quality Improvement

In the section entitled Concept and Measurement of Costs in chapter
4, we presented in some detail a procedure currently being widely used
to estimate the participation rates and benefits generated by new
lakes on reservoirs. The main idea was to use sample data from existing reservoirs to estimate participation rates as a function of such
population characteristics as income, population, travel costs, travel
time, and so on. When we assume that the participants would respond
to admission fees in the same way they would respond to added travel
costs, the participation function can be turned into a demand function
expressing the peoples' willingness to pay for the recreational use of
a new water body.

That model contained no water quality variable. One would expect a
positive response of water-based recreation to improvements in water
quality. For example, there is almost no recreational activity on the
estuary of the Delaware River. If water quality could be improved in
steps, there would be a response, probably first from boating, then
perhaps from fishing, and finally from swimming.

TABLE 19. Uniqueness Ratios for Aesthetic

Categories and factor No.	Site No.				
	1	2	3	4	5
Physical:					
1	0.14	0.14	0.14	0.14	0.33
2	.17	1.00	.50	.17	.33
3	1.00	.12	.12	.50	.12
4	.17	.17	.33	.17	.33
5	.11	.11	.50	.11	.11
6	.17	.17	.50	.17	.33
7	.10	.10	.10	1.00	.10
8	.10	.10	.10	1.00	.10
9	.20	.25	.20	.50	.25
10	.17	.17	.17	.33	.33
11	.20	.20	.17	.20	.17
12	.10	.10	.10	.10	.10
13	.10	.10	.10	.10	.10
14	.33	1.00	.50	.20	.50
Subtotal	3.06	3.73	3.53	4.69	3.20
Biologic:					
15	.50	.20	.50	1.00	.20
16	.17	.17	.17	.17	.25
17	.09	.09	.09	.09	.09
18	.20	.20	.33	.20	.33
19	.14	.14	.14	1.00	.33
20	.17	.17	.17	1.00	.50
21	.09	.09	.09	.09	.09
22	.09	.09	.09	.09	.09
23	.17	.17	.17	.17	.50
24	.14	.14	.14	.14	.50
25	.25	.50	.33	.33	.50
26	.33	.33	.17	.17	.33
27	.33	.17	.17	.50	.50
28	.25	.20	.25	.20	.20
Subtotal	2.92	2.66	2.81	5.15	4.41
Human interest:					
29	.20	.17	.20	.20	.17
30	.33	.17	.33	.33	.17
31	.11	.11	1.00	.50	.11
32	.08	.08	.08	.08	.08
33	.12	.12	.33	.12	1.00
34	.20	.20	.33	.20	.33
35	.20	.20	.50	.20	.50
36	.25	.25	.25	.33	.50
37	.25	.25	.25	.25	.50
38	.33	.50	.25	.33	.50
39	.17	.25	.17	.17	.25
40	1.00	.25	.25	.25	.25
41	.20	.20	.20	.20	.50
42	.50	.17	.50	.17	.50
43	.20	1.00	.20	.20	1.00
44	.33	.33	.33	.33	1.00
45	.50	.11	.11	.11	1.00
46	.12	.25	.25	.12	.12
Subtotal	5.09	4.61	5.53	4.09	8.48
Total	11.07	11.00	11.87	13.93	16.09

Table taken from Leopold

Since, as noted earlier in chapter 4, the benefits from water quality improvement to municipal and industrial water users appear to be
small, recreation plays a critical role in determining which programs
of water quality improvement are justifiable.

Two approaches could be taken to the measurement of recreational
benefits. The first approach isn't really a measurement at all, but
it helps in asking the right questions. This approach asks, Given what
we know about municipal and industrial benefits resulting from different (increasing) levels of water quality, how great will the

Factors at the Hells Canyon Sites

			Site No.			
6	7	8	9	10	11	12
0.50	0.50	0.14	0.33	0.33	0.14	0.14
.17	.17	.17	.33	.33	.17	.50
.50	1.00	.12	.12	.12	.12	.12
.17	.17	.33	.33	.33	.17	.33
.11	1.00	.11	.11	.11	.50	.11
.17	.17	.17	.33	.33	1.00	.50
.10	1.00	.10	.10	.10	.10	.10
.10	1.00	.10	.10	.10	.10	.10
.20	1.00	.25	.50	.25	.20	.20
.33	.17	.17	.33	.33	.33	.17
1.00	.20	.17	.17	.17	.20	.17
.10	1.00	1.00	.10	.10	.10	.10
.10	.50	.10	.10	.50	.10	.10
.20	1.00	.33	.33	.20	.20	.20
3.75	**8.88**	**3.26**	**3.28**	**3.30**	**3.43**	**2.84**
.50	.50	.20	.20	.50	.50	.20
.17	.50	.25	.25	.25	.17	.50
.09	1.00	.09	.09	.09	.09	.09
.33	1.00	.20	.20	.33	.33	.33
.33	1.00	.33	.14	.14	.14	.14
.33	.50	.33	.17	.33	.17	.17
.09	1.00	.09	.09	.09	.09	.09
.09	1.00	.09	.09	.09	.09	.09
.33	1.00	.33	.33	.17	.17	.50
.50	1.00	.50	.14	.14	.14	.50
.33	.25	1.00	.25	.25	.50	.50
.17	.33	.17	.33	.33	.17	.17
.17	.33	.33	.17	1.00	.17	.17
.20	.33	.33	.20	.25	.33	.25
3.67	**9.74**	**4.24**	**2.65**	**3.96**	**3.06**	**3.70**
.17	.17	1.00	.17	.17	.20	.20
.33	.17	.33	.17	.17	.33	.17
.11	.11	.50	.11	.11	.11	.11
.08	.08	.08	.08	.08	.08	.08
.12	.33	.12	.12	.12	.12	.33
.20	.33	.33	.33	1.00	.33	.20
.20	.33	.33	.33	.50	.50	.20
.33	.50	.25	.50	.50	1.00	.33
.25	.50	.50	.25	.50	.25	.25
.33	.33	.25	.25	.33	.33	.25
.17	.25	.17	.25	.50	.50	.17
.33	.25	.33	.33	.25	.25	.25
.20	.20	.20	.20	.50	.20	.20
.17	.17	1.00	.17	1.00	.50	.17
.20	.20	.20	.20	.20	.20	.33
.33	.33	.33	.50	.50	.33	.11
.11	.11	.11	.11	.50	.11	.11
.12	.12	.25	.25	.12	.12	.12
3.75	**4.48**	**6.28**	**4.32**	**7.05**	**5.46**	**3.67**
11.17	**23.10**	**13.78**	**10.25**	**14.31**	**11.95**	**10.21**

(1969, Table 3).

recreational benefits have to be to justify each level? Given the answers, one then asks, Which, if any, of those values is realistic or reasonable? Such an approach simply substitutes intuition for analysis, but this approach at least raises the right questions.

The second approach would be to develop an approach like that of the Texas study (chapter 4) and to include in the model as an explanatory variable the quality of the water (or perhaps several dimensions of water quality) of the various water bodies from which the sample data were collected. One could then estimate the population's

TABLE 20.   Summary-Totals of Uniqueness Ratios
of Aesthetic Factor Values, Hells Canyon Region

Site	Aesthetic factors			Total
	Physical	Biologic	Human interest	
1	3.06	2.92	5.09	11.07
2	3.73	2.66	4.61	11.00
3	3.53	2.81	5.53	11.87
4	4.69	5.15	4.09	13.93
5	3.20	4.41	8.48	16.09
6	3.75	3.67	3.75	11.17
7	8.88	9.74	4.48	23.10
8	3.26	4.24	6.28	13.78
9	3.28	2.65	4.32	10.25
10	3.30	3.96	7.05	14.31
11	3.43	3.06	5.46	11.95
12	2.84	3.70	3.67	10.21

Table taken from Leopold (1969, Table 4).

TABLE 21.   Sites in Order of Uniqueness Ratio

Rank	Aesthetic factors			Total
	Physical	Biologic	Human interest	
1	7	7	5	7
2	4	4	10	5
3	6	5	8	10
4	2	8	3	4
5	3	10	11	8
6	11	12	1	11
7	10	6	2	6
8	9	11	7	3
9	8	1	9	12
10	5	3	4	1
11	1	2	6	2
12	12	9	12	9

Table taken from Leopold (1969, Table 5).

willingness to pay for different water qualities by using the Clawson-Knetsch method.

Davidson et al. (1966) attempted an approach much like this for the Delaware Estuary. The basic functions comprising the heart of their analysis were (1) the 'proportion of population participating' functions for swimming, fishing, and boating, and (2) the 'amount of participation' functions indicating the number of days a particular type of participant was likely to spend in the sport annually. The general idea was that both types of functions might have water quality variables in them so that, given the population characteristics of the Delaware Estuary region, the total number of recreation days for each type of sport could be estimated as a function of water quality.

TABLE 22. Downstream Municipal Intake Water Treatment
Savings as a Percentage of Increased Upstream Sewage
Treatment Costs for Various Degrees of Sewage Treatment

Amount of Upstream Discharge, mgd	Distance to Downstream Intake, miles	Type of Sewage Treatment Change		
		Raw to Primary	Primary to HRTF*	HRTF* to Tertiary
2.5	5	negligible	0.04	0.02
	10	negligible	0.03	0.02
	20	negligible	0.03	0.01
	50	negligible	0.01	0.02
10.0	5	negligible	0.10	0.05
	10	negligible	0.10	0.04
	20	negligible	0.08	0.04
	50	negligible	0.07	0.03

Table adapted from Frankel (1965, Table 4). Table based on municipal withdrawals of 2.5 mgd and the hydrology of the Eel River, California.
 * HRTF (high rate trickling filter).

Future recreation days (like dollars) could be discounted back to the present and valued at a common value for each sport. Then a curve relating the present value of recreation benefits to water quality could be superimposed on a curve relating water quality to costs. This curve permitted the determination of that water quality level at which incremental recreational benefits just equal the incremental costs of achieving that level of water quality.

Naturally, this approach as carried out leaves unanswered the question of the value to be placed on a day of swimming, fishing, or boating. In this approach, alternative benefit curves for different values of a day's recreation are constructed. There are then several intersection points, and one is left again with the question, Is $2.50 (or $5, or whatever) a reasonable value to place on a day's recreation?

The functions used by Davidson et al. were estimated from University of Michigan Survey Research Center data of 1352 households from different parts of the country. Water quality, represented by an expert's evaluation of the quality of the site for recreational

purposes, appeared as a significant explanatory variable in only one
of the proportion of population functions, strangely the one for boating. The reason may have been the inappropriateness of the data or
perhaps a narrow range of variation in the measure of water quality.
The authors then continued the analysis by assuming that boating would
take place at the level predicted by the model if water quality were
brought up to 3 ppm dissolved oxygen (DO), that fishing would take
place as predicted if the DO were raised to 4 ppm, and that swimming
would take place as predicted if the DO were raised to 5 ppm.

Clearly, much more work on the relationship between water quality
and participation in water-based recreation needs to be done. Dissolved oxygen alone certainly is inadequate as a measure of water
quality. The dimensions of water quality that people perceive as important must be known, as well as the appropriate standards from a
health viewpoint. Work on the public's perception of water quality
has been done by White and Strodebeck (unpublished manuscript, 1968)
and David (1971).

Management and Financing of Water Quality Programs

There are many ways in which the task of achieving a given set of
water quality standards can be divided among polluters and between
polluters and centralized waste treatment facilities.

Perhaps the most widely applied procedure to date for raising water
quality standards is to require all waste dischargers to reduce their
waste loads by the same percentage. This procedure, uniform cutback,
is often thought of as being equitable or fair. It clearly is ineffi-
cient regarding cost, for the costs of achieving a given percentage
cutback will differ greatly from polluter to polluter. It certainly
isn't clear that this procedure represents fairness.

One could compare the costs of this traditional approach with a
minimum cost solution whereby each polluter is assigned a particular
amount of waste discharge reduction, the amount being determined by
the condition that incremental waste reduction costs be the same for
all polluters. If centralized treatment facilities are available,
then incremental private waste reduction costs should also equal the

incremental costs of reduction through centralized treatment. The
execution of such a scheme requires that the management body know all
the private waste reduction cost functions. This scheme can result in
radically different degrees of treatment at different points, depending on cost differences and the dynamics of the pollution pattern.

A third device that has received a great deal of attention is the
use of effluent charges on polluters as a device for motivating the
reduction of waste loads. The assumption is that any polluter faced
with a charge of X cents per unit of waste discharged to the stream
(or central treatment plant) will cut back on his discharges as long
as he can do so at costs of less than X cents per unit. As the effluent charges are raised, cutbacks on discharges will be larger. Thus
a water quality authority presumably could find some set of effluent
charges (for the different waste materials) that would achieve the
desired set of stream quality standards.

The dynamics of the pollution pattern (e.g., the oxygen sag, the
dilution of toxic materials, the adsorption of materials on silts, and
so on) usually make discharges at some points more critical than at
other points. It might, therefore, be appropriate to impose different
sets of effluent charges in different reaches of the river. Such a
scheme is referred to as the zoned effluent charge.

Johnson (1967) studied the application of these four schemes (uniform treatment, least cost, single effluent charge, and zoned effluent
charge) to the achievement of alternative dissolved oxygen standards
in the Delaware Estuary. Johnson's study coupled a large computer
model for forecasting DO conditions in various parts of the estuary
with a linear programing procedure for determining the way to achieve
minimum cost under each scheme. To compare the cost implications of
each scheme, we present in Table 23 partial numerical results from
Johnson's study.

As a result of that study, Johnson concludes that effluent charges
should be given much more serious consideration as a pollution control
tool. The major advantages of effluent charge schemes are:

1. they can approximate a least cost solution to the achievement
of given standards;

TABLE 23.   Total Costs of Waste Removal for
Alternative Methods of Achieving Specified DO Goal,
Delaware Estuary (Cost in 10^6/year)

DO Goal, ppm	Uniform Treatment	Single Effluent Charge	Zone Effluent Charge	Least Cost Solution
2	5.0	2.5	2.5	1.6
3	11.2	7.7	7.4	6.9
4	723.0	723.0	723.0	716.0

Table adapted from Johnson (1967, Table 2).   These
figures assume no prior sludge removal from the bottom
and are predicated upon a particular reaeration rate.

2.   they produce a continuing incentive for waste dischargers to
seek ways of reducing waste streams;

3.   they produce a continuing source of revenue for the water pollution program;

4.   they appear to be far more equitable than other schemes.

Upton (1971) has considered some of the financial implications of
combining effluent charges with centralized treatment in the attempt
to achieve specified standards at minimum cost.   Working with a model
of Ohio's Miami River basin, Upton found that optimum effluent charges
imposed on the various polluters would yield revenues to the water
control authority sufficient to pay only 85% of the costs of the optimum centralized treatment plant.

A deficit of this magnitude might not be legally or politically
feasible for some agencies and might possibly preclude the use of the
minimum cost program.   A question then arises concerning the increase
in overall costs of achieving the stream standards if polluters were
charged not the optimum effluent charge (i.e., the incremental cost of
centralized treatment per pound of waste) but an amount equaling the
average cost of centralized treatment, i.e., an amount sufficient to
cover all the treatment plant costs.   In the case of the Miami basin,
this modified form of the effluent charge added only 1% to overall
costs.   Whereas it is difficult to know how much one can generalize
from this result, it suggests that setting effluent charges equal to

the average costs of centralized treatment may not represent a major departure from the minimum cost solution in situations where individual polluters, industries, and towns can be coupled to regional treatment plants.

REFERENCES

Arrow, K. J., and R. C. Lind, Uncertainty and the evaluation of public investment decisions, *Amer. Econ. Rev.*, *60*, 1970.

Brown, W. G., An economic evaluation of the Oregon salmon and steelhead sport fishery, *Tech. Bull. 78*, Oreg. State Agr. Exp. Sta., Corvallis, 1964.

Cesario, F. J., and J. L. Knetsch, Time bias in recreation benefit estimates, *Water Resour. Res.*, *6*(3), 700-704, 1970.

Clawson, M., and J. L. Knetsch, *Economics of Outdoor Recreation*, Johns Hopkins Press for Resources for the Future, Baltimore, Md., 1966.

David, E. L., Public perceptions of water quality, *Water Resour. Res.*, *7*(3), 453-457, 1971.

Davidson, P., G. F. Adams, and J. Seneca, The social value of water recreational facilities resulting from an improvement in water quality: The Delaware Estuary, in *Water Research*, edited by A. V. Kneese and S. C. Smith, Johns Hopkins Press, Baltimore, Md., 1966.

Davis, R. K., The value of outdoor recreation: An economic study of the Maine woods, Ph.D. thesis, Harvard Univ., Cambridge, Mass., 1963.

Davis, R. K., The value of big game hunting in a private forest, in *Transactions of the 29th North American Wildlife and Natural Resources Conference*, pp. 393-403, Wildlife Management Institute, Washington, D. C., 1964.

Davis, R. K., *The Range of Choice in Water Management: A Study of Dissolved Oxygen in the Potomac Estuary*, Johns Hopkins Press for Resources for the Future, Baltimore, Md., 1968.

Fiering, M. B, and B. Jackson, *Synthetic Streamflows*, AGU, Washington, D. C., 1971.

Frankel, R. J., Water quality management: Engineering-economic factors in municipal waste disposal, *Water Resour. Res.*, *1*(2), 173-186, 1965.

Freeman, A. M., III, Six federal reclamation projects and the distribution of income, *Water Resour. Res.*, *3*(2), 319-332, 1967.

Freeman, A. M., III, and R. H. Haveman, Benefit-cost analysis and multiple objectives: Current issues in water resources planning, *Water Resour. Res.*, *6*(6), 1533-1539, 1970.

Grubb, H. W., and J. T. Goodwin, Economic evaluation of water-oriented recreation in the preliminary Texas water plan, *Rep. 84*, Tex. Water Develop. Board, Austin, 1968.

Hanke, S. H., Demand for water under dynamic conditions, *Water Resour. Res.*, *6*(5), 1253-1261, 1970.

Haveman, R. H., *Water Resource Investment and the Public Interest,* Vanderbilt University Press, Nashville, Tenn., 1965.

Haveman, R. H., The opportunity cost of displaced private spending and the social discount rate, *Water Resour. Res.*, *5*(5), 947-957, 1969.

Haveman, R. H., *Ex Post Analysis of Water Resource Projects,* Johns Hopkins Press, Baltimore, Md., 1971.

Haveman, R. H., and J. V. Krutilla, *Unemployment, Idle Capacity, and the Evaluation of Public Expenditures: National and Regional Analyses,* Johns Hopkins Press, Baltimore, Md., 1968.

Howe, C. W., Water resources and regional economic growth in the United States, 1950-1960, *S. Econ. J.*, *34*(4), 1968a.

Howe, C. W., Water pricing in residential areas, *J. Amer. Water Works Ass.*, *60*(5), 1968b.

Howe, C. W., and K. W. Easter, *Interbasin Transfers of Water: Economic Issues and Impacts,* Johns Hopkins Press for Resources for the Future, Baltimore, Md., 1971.

Howe, C. W., and F. P. Linaweaver, Jr., The impact of price on residential water demand and its relation to system design and price structure, *Water Resour. Res.*, *3*(1), 13-32, 1967.

Howe, C. W., et al., *Inland Waterway Transportation: Studies in Public and Private Management and Investment Decisions,* Johns Hopkins Press for Resources for the Future, Baltimore, Md., 1969.

James, L. D., A case study in income redistribution from reservoir construction, *Water Resour. Res.*, *4*(3), 499-508, 1968.

James, I. C., B. T. Bower, and N. C. Matalas, Relative importance of variables in water resources planning, *Water Resour. Res.*, *5*(6), 1165-1173, 1969.

Johnson, E. L., A study in the economics of water quality management, *Water Resour. Res.*, *3*(2), 291-306, 1967.

Kalter, R. J., and L. E. Gosse, *Outdoor Recreation in New York State: Projections of Demand, Economic Value, and Pricing Effects, Cornell Univ. Agr. Exp. Sta. Spec. Ser.,* vol. 5, Cornell University, Ithaca, N. Y., 1969.

Kalter, R. J., et al., Federal evaluation of resource investments: A case study, *Agr. Econ. Res. Bull. 313,* Cornell Univ. Water Resour. Center and Dep. of Agr. Econ., Ithaca, N. Y., 1970.

Kneese, A. V., and B. T. Bower, *Managing Water Quality: Economics, Technology, Institutions,* Johns Hopkins Press, Baltimore, Md., 1968.

Krutilla, J. V., *The Columbia River Treaty: The Economics of an International River Basin Development,* Johns Hopkins Press, Baltimore, Md., 1967a.

Krutilla, J. V., Conservation reconsidered, *Amer. Econ. Rev.*, *57*(4), 777-786, 1967b.

Leopold, L. B., Quantitative comparison of some aesthetic factors among rivers, *U.S. Geol. Surv. Circ. 620*, Washington, D. C., 1969.

Leopold, L. B., and M. O'Brien Marchand, On the quantitative inventory of the riverscape, *Water Resour. Res.*, *4*(4), 709-718, 1968.

Litton, B. R., Jr., Landscape and esthetic quality, in *America's Changing Environment*, edited by R. Revelle and H. H. Landsberg, Houghton Mifflin, Boston, Mass., 1970.

Marglin, S. A., *Public Investment Criteria: Benefit-Cost Analysis for Planned Economic Growth*, MIT Press, Cambridge, Mass., 1968.

Moore, C. V., and T. R. Hedges, Economics of on-farm irrigation water availability and costs and related farm adjustments: Farm size in relation to resource use, earnings, and adjustments on the San Joaquin eastside, *Res. Rep.263*, Calif. Agr. Exp. Sta., Giannini Found. of Agr. Econ., Berkeley, 1963.

Olson, M., Jr., The optimal allocation of jurisdictional responsibility: The principle of 'fiscal equivalence,' in *The Analysis and Evaluation of Public Expenditures: The PPB System*, vol. 1, A compendium of papers submitted to the Subcommittee on Economy in Government, pp. 321, 331, U.S. Joint Economic Committee, Washington, D. C., 1969.

Parker, D. S., and J. A. Crutchfield, Water quality management and the time profile of benefits and costs, *Water Resour. Res.*, *4*(2), 233-246, 1968.

Pincock, M. G. Assessing impacts of declining water quality on gross value output of agriculture, A case study, *Water Resour. Res.*, *5*(1), 1-12, 1969.

Riordan, C., General multistage marginal cost dynamic programing model for the optimization of a class of investment pricing decisions, *Water Resour. Res.*, *7*(2), 245-253, 1971a.

Riordan, C., A multistage marginal cost model of investment-pricing decisions: Application to urban water supply treatment facilities, *Water Resour. Res.*, *7*(3), 463-478, 1971b.

Russell, C. S., D. Arey, and R. Kates, *Drought and Water Supply: Lessons of the Massachusetts Experience for Municipal Planning*, Johns Hopkins Press, Baltimore, Md., 1971.

Schmid, A. A., and W. Ward, A test of federal water project evaluation procedures with emphasis on regional income and environmental quality: Detroit River, Trenton navigation channel, *Agr. Econ. Rep. 158*, Mich. State Univ., East Lansing, April 1970.

Schramm, G., and R. E. Burt, Jr., *An Analysis of Federal Water Resource Planning and Evaluation Procedures*, School of Natural Resources, University of Michigan, Ann Arbor, June 1970.

Teller, A., Air pollution abatement: An economic study into the cost of control, Ph.D. thesis, Johns Hopkins University, Baltimore, Md., 1966.

Teller, A., Air pollution abatement: Economic rationality and reality, in *America's Changing Environment*, edited by R. Revelle and H. H. Landsberg, Houghton Mifflin, Boston, Mass., 1970.

U.S. Army Corps of Engineers, *Plan of Study, Susquehanna River Basin Study*, U.S. Army Engineer District, Baltimore, Md., September 1965.

U.S. Congress, Economic analysis of public investment decisions: Interest rate policy and discounting analysis, Joint Economic Committee, 90th Congress, 2nd Session, 1968.

U.S. Department of the Army, *Susquehanna River Basin Study Plan: A Review of Alternatives*, Washington, D. C., November 30, 1966.

U.S. Interagency Committee on Water Resources, *Proposed Practices for Economic Analysis of River Basin Projects* (the 'Green Book'), Washington, D. C., May 1950. (Revised May 1958.)

U.S. Water Resources Council, *Report to the Water Resources Council by the Special Task Force: Principles for Planning Water and Land Resources*, Washington, D. C., July 1970a.

U.S. Water Resources Council, *Report to the Water Resources Council by the Special Task Force: Standards for Planning Water and Land Resources*, Washington, D. C., July 1970b.

U.S. Water Resources Council, *Report to the Water Resources Council by the Special Task Force: Findings and Recommendations*, Washington, D. C., July 1970c.

U.S. Water Resources Council, *Report to the Water Resources Council by the Special Task Force: A Summary Analysis of Nineteen Tests of Proposed Evaluation Procedures on Selected Water and Land Resource Projects*, Washington, D. C., July 1970d.

Upton, C., Application of user charges to water quality management, *Water Resour. Res.*, *7*(2), 264-272, 1971.

Weisbrod, B. A., Income redistribution effects and benefit cost analysis, in *Problems in Public Expenditure Analysis*, edited by S. B. Chase, Jr., The Brookings Institution, Washington, D. C., 1968.

Werner, R. R., An investigation of the employment of multiple objectives in water resources planning, Ph.D. thesis, South Dakota State University, Brookings, 1968.

NOTES

NOTES